Worshiping the Beloved

al-Burāq Publications

Copyright

ISBN: 978-1-956276-41-1
Printed and published by al-Burāq Publications.
Translated and annotated by al-Burāq Publications. Where needed, context and transliterations were added. Some minor edits were made to the translated Arabic text.

Ordering Information
We offer discounts and promotions for wholesale purchases, non-profit organizations, and other educational institutions. Contact us at the email below for further information.

www.al-Buraq.org
publications@al-Buraq.org

First Edition | June 2023

Dedication

The publication of this book was made possible through the generous support of our donors.

Please recite *Sūrat al-Fātihah* and ask God for the Divine reward (*thawāb*) to be conferred upon the donors and also the souls of all the deceased in whose memory their loved ones have contributed graciously towards the publication of *Worshiping the Beloved.*

We begin by giving all praise and thanks to God ﷻ for giving us the *tawfīq* to translate this book. He has guided us and without Him, we would not have been guided to the straight path embodied by the Prophet Muḥammad ﷺ and the Ahl al-Bayt عليهم السلام.

This book is dedicated to all the scholars, martyrs and believers who worked tirelessly to promote the pure Muḥammadan path.

We want to also give our thanks and appreciation to all believers from around the world and acknowledge the team which helped al-Burāq Publications complete this work, spending countless hours to make its publication possible. Please recite Sūrat al-Fātiḥah on behalf of them, their families, and their marḥūmīn.

This book is dedicated in honor of the following individuals. Please remember them in your prayers and may God ﷻ have mercy on them and their loved ones.

Alena Viktorovna

Ali Ftouni

Ali Khoyee

Aliya Haider

Alya Agemy

Amal Sulais

Anees Rizvi

Bande Khuda

Batoul Hijazi

Faisal H. Khalil

Falah Khachan

Fidahussein Rajani

Ghazwa Debouk

Hajj Abd Al Sada Al Barak

Hajj Ahmad Sheet

Hajj Deeb Aoun

Hajj Hassan Sobh

Hajj Nabih H. Kobeissi

Hajj Sami Ftouni

Hajji Amneh Sobh-Ftouni

Hajji Hiam Hojeije

Hajji Imane Srour

Hajji Murad

Khalaf Hafedh

Kisma Mingash

Lina Sabah

Mahammedali Hassan

Mahmoud Tiba

Misale K. Bazzi

Mohamed Awada

Mohammad A. Jafri

Mohammed Hafedh

Mohammed R. Hafedh

Moosa H. Shafaei

Muslimah Bilal

N Nasser

Nafees Khan

Naji Mujahid

Naseer Khan

Nusrat Zahra Shah

Omar Al-Bugis

Oussama N. Kobeissi

Rohia Awada

Rukaya Hassan

Sajida Fatima

Sayed Ghaleb Al Musawi

Hajji Sabah Atwi

Hajji Sobhia Aoun

Hajji Zahya Fawaz

Hassan Hassan

Huda Hassan

Hussein Diab

Hussein Hassan

Ibtisam Hammoud

Jannah S. Abidi

Kaltham Qasim

Kassim Awada

Sayed Nebras Al Musawi

Sayed Taleb K. Al Musawi

Sayyid Sobh H. Sobh

Shahīd Ibrāhīm Hādī

Sherali Rizvi

Syed Mujtaba H. Rizvi

Taleb Sabah

Turfah Sobh

Zahra T Sabah

Zahra W. Ahmad

Duʿāʾ al-Ḥujjah

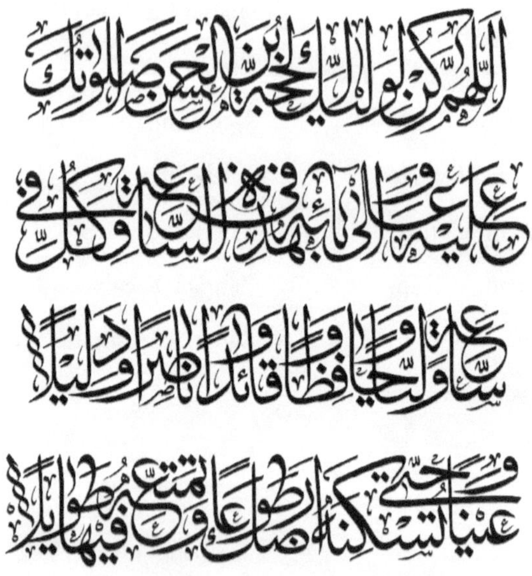

O God, be, for Your representative, the Ḥujjat (proof), son of al-Ḥasan, Your blessings be upon him and his forefathers, in this hour and in every hour: a guardian, a protector, a leader, a helper, a proof, and an eye - until You make him live on the Earth, in obedience (to You), and cause him to live in it for a long time.

Terms of Respect

The following Arabic phrases have been used throughout this book in their respective places to show the reverence which the noble personalities deserve.

Used for God, meaning:
Exalted and Sublime (Perfect) is He

Used for Prophet Muḥammad, meaning:
Blessings from God be upon him and his family

Used for a man (singular) of a high status, meaning:
Peace be upon him

Used for a woman (singular) of a high status, meaning:
Peace be upon her

Used for men/women (dual) of a high status, meaning:
Peace be upon them both

Used for men and/or women (plural) of a high status, meaning:
Peace be upon them all

Used for Imām Muḥammad al-Mahdī, meaning:
May God hasten his return

Used for a deceased scholar, meaning:
May his resting [burial] place remain pure

Transliteration Table

The method of transliteration of Islamic terminology from the Arabic language has been carried out according to the standard transliteration table below.

ء	ʾ	ر	r	ف	f
ا	a	ز	z	ق	q
ب	b	س	s	ك	k
ت	t	ش	sh	ل	l
ث	th	ص	ṣ	م	m
ج	j	ض	ḍ	ن	n
ح	ḥ	ط	ṭ	و	w
خ	kh	ظ	ẓ	ه	h
د	d	ع	ʿ	ي	y
ذ	dh	غ	gh		

Long Vowels					
ا	ā	و	ū	ي	ī

Short Vowels					
◌َ	a	◌ُ	u	◌ِ	i

Table of Contents

Introduction

In the Name of God, the Beneficent, the Merciful

Praise be to God, the Lord of all worlds, and may He send blessings and salutations upon our master Muḥammad ﷺ and his pure family ﷺ.

The status of a person can only be valued based on how much he worships God ﷻ and is connected to Him ﷻ. Only by doing this can a person achieve the state that he is meant to reach, becoming a manifestation of the verse:

﴿وَما خَلَقتُ الجِنَّ وَالإِنسَ إِلّا لِيَعبُدونِ﴾

﴿wa-mā khalaqtu l-jinna wa-l-ʾinsa ʾillā li-yaʿbudūni﴾

﴿I did not create the jinn and the humans except that they may worship Me﴾[1]

This is not limited to praying, fasting, and other acts of worship. It also depends on the person's thoughts, intentions, and relationships with those

---

[1] Sūrat al-Dhāriyāt, Verse 56.

around him. All these things must be dedicated to the Creator ﷻ and based on what He loves and is pleased with. A person's purpose in any good deed must be gaining His ﷻ pleasure and nearness.

There are many manifestations of true worshipfulness. For this reason, we have chosen to include some topics related to worship in this book, explaining them easily and straightforwardly based on the Noble Qur'ān and the noble sunnah. We intend to offer this material to the noble scholars and preachers of Islam, hoping it will be a helpful resource when preaching and spreading Islam. We ask our Master ﷻ to grant us all success so that we may be honest worshipful servants and accept our and your good deeds.

The Purpose of Creation

The goal of the chapter is to know the primary purpose of creation and reorienting our relationship to this world through understanding the following:

1. The universe is created with wisdom and purpose.

2. The Islamic view on the purpose of creation.

3. The following verse:

﴿وَابْتَغِ فِيمَا آتَاكَ اللَّهُ الدَّارَ الآخِرَةَ وَلا تَنسَ نَصِيبَكَ مِنَ الدُّنيا﴾

*﴾wa-btaghi fī-mā ʾātāka llāhu d-dāra l-ʾākhirata
wa-lā tansa naṣībaka mina d-dunyā﴿*

*﴾By the means of what God has given you, seek the
abode of the Hereafter, while not forgetting your
share of this world﴿*[2]

4. Blameworthy diversions (*lahw*) and purposeful diversions.

Imām ʿAlī ﷺ: "When God created the creation, He did not need their obedience, and He was secure from their disobedience. The disobedience of those

---

[2] Sūrat al-Qaṣaṣ, Verse 77.

who disobey him does not harm Him, and the obedience of those who obey Him does not benefit Him."[3]

Someone may think that the acts and righteous deeds that the pious perform and the virtuous qualities and praiseworthy acts that lead to divine nearness that God ﷻ requires are things that God ﷻ needs. For this reason, the Imām ﷺ began his sermon on the pious with the above words. He ﷺ alerted people that God ﷻ is free from such a description and above deficit and need. The Imām ﷺ explains that God's ﷻ purpose behind creation and existence was not to bring a benefit upon Himself or drive away harm like humans do. God is the Living One, the Sustainer, who is absolute in His essence, attributes, and actions:

﴿يَا أَيُّهَا النَّاسُ أَنتُمُ الفُقَرَاءُ إِلَى اللَّهِ ۖ وَاللَّهُ هُوَ الغَنِيُّ الحَمِيدُ﴾

⟨yā-'ayyuhā n-nāsu 'antumu l-fuqarā'u 'ilā llāhi wa-llāhu huwa l-ghaniyyu l-ḥamīdᵘ⟩

---

[3] Sharīf Raḍī, Muḥammad b. al-Ḥusayn, *Nahj al-Balāgha (Khuṭab al-Imām ʿAlī)*, ed. and corr. Ṣubḥī al-Ṣāliḥ. n.p. Beirut: Lebanon, 1387/1967, 1st ed., p. 303.

❪*O mankind! You are the ones who stand in need of God, and God—He is the Sufficient, the Laudable*❫[4]

The Universe Is Created With Wisdom and Purpose

God ﷻ says,

﴿وَما خَلَقْنَا السَّماءَ وَالأَرضَ وَما بَيْنَهُما لاعِبينَ﴾

❪*wa-mā khalaqnā s-samāʾa wa-l-ʾarḍa wa-mā baynahumā lāʿibīnᵃ*❫

﴿لَو أَرَدنا أَن نَتَّخِذَ لَهوًا لَاتَّخَذناهُ مِن لَدُنّا إِن كُنّا فاعِلينَ﴾

❪*law ʾaradnā ʾan nattakhidha lahwan la-ttakhadhnāhu min ladunnā ʾin kunnā fāʿilīnᵃ*❫

﴿بَل نَقذِفُ بِالحَقِّ عَلَى الباطِلِ فَيَدمَغُهُ فَإِذا هُوَ زاهِقٌ ۚ وَلَكُمُ الوَيلُ مِمّا تَصِفونَ﴾

❪*bal naqdhifu bi-l-ḥaqqi ʿalā l-bāṭili fa-yadmaghuhū fa-ʾidhā huwa zāhiqun wa-lakumu l-waylu mimmā taṣifūnᵃ*❫

---

[4] Sūrat Fāṭir, Verse 15.

❨We did not create the sky and the earth and whatever is between them for play. Had We desired to take up some diversion We would have surely taken it up with Ourselves, were We to do [so]. Rather We hurl the truth against falsehood, and it crushes its head, and behold, falsehood vanishes! And woe to you for what you allege [about God]❩[5]

God ﷻ created creation while He was self-sufficient and transcendent from needing them. This does not mean that creation was aimless; aimlessness contradicts divine wisdom. God ﷻ said,

$$\text{﴿أَفَحَسِبْتُمْ أَنَّمَا خَلَقْنَاكُمْ عَبَثًا وَأَنَّكُمْ إِلَيْنَا لَا تُرْجَعُونَ﴾}$$

❨ʾa-fa-ḥasibtum ʾannamā khalaqnākum ʿabathan wa-ʾannakum ʾilaynā lā turjaʿūnᵃ❩

❨Did you suppose that We created you aimlessly, and that you will not be brought back to Us?❩[6]

"Aimless" describes something with no real purpose and is the opposite of wisdom. The negation in "and that you will not be brought back

---

[5] Sūrat al-Anbiyāʾ, Verses 16-18.

[6] Sūrat al-Muʾminūn, Verse 115.

to Us?'"[7] means that people thought that there was no wisdom behind their creation.

Any action must be done for a specific goal; naturally, the goal behind sending prophets ﷺ was the perfection of humankind. Religions have stated that prophets were sent to help man and aid him in reaching perfection.

Human life suffers from a lack and a defect that cannot be fixed, individually or with the help of other ordinary members of society. For this reason, man should seek the help of revelation.

The Goal of Creation: The Islamic Vision

God ﷻ asks, "Does man suppose he has been abandoned to futility?"[8] What is the purpose of creation? God ﷻ said,

﴿وَمَا خَلَقْتُ الْجِنَّ وَالْإِنسَ إِلَّا لِيَعْبُدُونِ﴾

﴿wa-mā khalaqtu l-jinna wa-l-'insa 'illā li-ya'budūni﴾

---

[7] Ibid.

[8] Sūrat al-Qiyāmah, Verse 36.

*❨I did not create the jinn and the humans
except that they may worship Me❩*[9]

This means that worship is the purpose behind the creation of the Jinn and the humans. What does this goal mean, and what is the point of worship?

From Ibn Abī 'Umayr, he said, "I said to Abū al-Ḥasan Mūsā b. Ja'far, 'What does the saying of the Prophet ﷺ, 'Go on working, for each creature is aided in the purpose that it was created for' mean?' He said, 'God created the Jinn and humans to worship Him. He did not create them to disobey Him. That is the meaning of God's saying, 'I did not create the jinn and the humans except that they may worship Me.'[10] God aided each creature in the purpose that He created them for. Woe to those who prefer blindness to guidance!'"[11]

From Imām Ja'far al-Ṣādiq ﷺ: "Imām al-Ḥusayn b. 'Alī ﷺ went to his companions and said, 'God only created His servants so they may know Him. If

---

[9] Sūrat al-Dhāriyāt, Verse 56.

[10] Ibid.

[11] Majlisī, 'Allamah Muḥammad Bāqir, *Biḥār al-Anwār al-Jāmi'a li-Durar al-A'imma al-Aṭhār*, Beirut: Mu'assasat al-Wafā', 1403/1983, 2nd ed., Vol. 5, p. 157.

they knew Him, they would worship Him, and if they worship Him, that will suffice them from worshiping anyone other than Him."[12]

Many verses in the Noble Qurʾān contain allusions to the purpose behind creating a man or the universe. These allusions may seem different, but if we look closely, we will notice that they refer to one truth. These allusions include the following.

1. Worship: God ﷻ said, "I did not create the jinn and the humans except that they may worship Me."[13]

2. Testing people: God ﷻ said,

$$\text{﴿وَهُوَ الَّذِي خَلَقَ السَّمَاوَاتِ وَالْأَرْضَ فِي سِتَّةِ أَيَّامٍ وَكَانَ عَرْشُهُ عَلَى الْمَاءِ لِيَبْلُوَكُمْ أَيُّكُمْ أَحْسَنُ عَمَلًا﴾}$$

❨wa-huwa lladhī khalaqa s-samāwāti wa-l-ʾarḍa fī sittati ʾayyāmin wa-kāna ʿarshuhū ʿalā l-māʾi li-yabluwakum ʾayyukum ʾaḥsanu ʿamalan❩

---

12 Ibid., Vol. 5, p. 312.

13 Sūrat al-Dhāriyāt, Verse 56.

❰It is He who created the heavens and the earth in six days —and His Throne was [then] upon the waters — that He may test you [to see] which of you is best in conduct❱14

3.   Divine mercy:

﴿إِلَّا مَن رَّحِمَ رَبُّكَ ۚ وَلِذَٰلِكَ خَلَقَهُمْ﴾

❰illā man raḥima rabbuka wa-li-dhālika khalaqahum❱

❰except those on whom your Lord has mercy —and that is why He created them❱15

4.   Learning and knowledge of God's ﷻ attributes:

﴿اللَّهُ الَّذِي خَلَقَ سَبْعَ سَمَاوَاتٍ وَمِنَ الْأَرْضِ مِثْلَهُنَّ يَتَنَزَّلُ الْأَمْرُ بَيْنَهُنَّ لِتَعْلَمُوا أَنَّ اللَّهَ عَلَىٰ كُلِّ شَيْءٍ قَدِيرٌ وَأَنَّ اللَّهَ قَدْ أَحَاطَ بِكُلِّ شَيْءٍ عِلْمًا﴾

❰allāhu lladhī khalaqa sabʿa samāwātin wa-mina l-ʾarḍi mithlahunna yatanazzalu l-ʾamru baynahunna li-taʿlamū ʾanna llāha ʿalā kulli

---

14 Sūrat Hūd, Verse 7.

15 Sūrat Hūd, Verse 119.

shay'in qadīrun wa-'anna llāha
qad 'aḥāṭa bi-kulli shay'in 'ilma^n⟩

⟨*It is God who has created seven heavens, and of the
earth [a number] similar to them. The command
gradually descends through them, that you may
know that God has power over all things, and that
God comprehends all things in knowledge*⟩[16]

Even a little contemplation of these verses shows us
that some of them are precedents to others.
Knowledge is a precedent for worship, and worship
is a precedent for testing and human perfection,
and testing and human perfection are precedents
for benefitting from God's ﷻ mercy.

The purpose of our creation is our perfection and
elevation, which happens through our knowledge
of our Creator and our worship of or obedience to
Him. By obeying God ﷻ, we grow more perfect
and walk the path of wisdom (*ḥikma*), and by
disobeying Him, we sink toward animality, lust,
vain talk (*laghū*), and purposelessness.

---

[16] Sūrat al-Ṭalāq, Verse 12.

Not Forgetting Your Share of This World

What we said earlier about the purposefulness behind the creation of humankind and obedience and worship being the basis of human life does not mean that we must only look to what is beyond the world. Islam is a religion that mimics man's nature (*tabī'a*) and natural disposition (*fiṭra*) and gives everything its proper dues. Man has a material side that must be taken into consideration. If it is not taken into consideration at all, this will lead to an adverse reaction. Imām 'Alī ﷺ says, "Give your hearts a break, for if they are forced to do things, they will become blind."[17] He also narrated it ﷺ: "The hearts have an appetite and an activity and a decline. Approach them according to their appetite and activity, for if the heart is forced to do something, it becomes blind."[18]

---

[17] Al-Aḥsā'ī, Ibn Abī Jumhūr, *'Awālī al-La'ālī al-'Azīziyya fil-Aḥādīth al-Dīniyya*, ed. Ḥajj Aqā Mujtabā al-'Irāqī, Dār Sayyid al-Shuhadā' lil-Nashr, Qom: Iran, 1403/1983, 1st ed., Vol. 3, p. 296.

[18] Sharīf Raḍī, Muḥammad b. al-Ḥusayn, *Nahj al-Balāgha*, ed. Ṣāliḥ, 503.

Blameworthy and Purposeful Diversions

God ﷻ says,

﴿وَما هٰذِهِ الْحَياةُ الدُّنيا إِلّا لَهوٌ وَلَعِبٌ ۚ وَإِنَّ الدّارَ الآخِرَةَ لَهِيَ الحَيَوانُ ۚ لَو كانوا يَعلَمونَ﴾

‹wa-mā hādhihi l-ḥayātu d-dunyā ʾillā lahwun wa-laʿibun wa-ʾinna d-dāra l-ʾākhirata la-hiya l-ḥayawānu law kānū yaʿlamūn[a]›

‹*The life of this world is nothing but diversion and play, but the abode of the Hereafter is indeed Life, had they known!*›[19]

Diversion is any action that distracts man from the primary aspects of life. As for play, it is a name for all actions involving some imaginative system and goal. During the play, for example, one person pretends to be a king, the other pretends to be a minister, the third pretends to be an army commander, and the fourth pretends to be a thief. After this playtime slot is over, everything goes back to the ordinary.

---

[19] Sūrat al-ʿAnkabūt, Verse 64.

Some narrations criticize vain diversions that cause a person to forget his serious responsibilities. The Commander of the Believers ﷻ said, "Diversion is one of the fruits of ignorance."[20] And "Those who are overly fond of play and heedless because of diversion and amusement will never become sensible."[21] On the other hand, some ḥadīths point out the existence of a purposeful diversion that believers engage in to raise their spirits. The Prophet ﷺ said, "Take up archery, for it is the best of your diversions."[22]

This means that the believer should be severe and wise in life but without turning away from life and the cultivation of it.

---

[20] al-Laythī al-Wāsiṭī, Shaykh Kāfī al-Dīn ʿAlī b. Muḥammad, *ʿUyūn al-Ḥikam wal-Mawāʿiẓ*, ed. Shaykh Ḥusayn al-Ḥusaynī al-Bīrjandī, Qom: Dār al-Ḥadīth, 1418, 1st ed., p. 61.

[21] Ibid., p. 414.

[22] al-Muttaqī al-Hindī, ʿAlāʾ al-Dīn ʿAlī al-Muttaqī b. Ḥusām al-Dīn, *Kanz al-ʿUmmāl fī Sunan al-Aqwāl wal-Afʿāl*, ed. And comm. Shaykh Bakrī Ḥayyānī, corr. Shaykh Ṣafwat al-Saqqā, Muʾassasat al-Risāla, n.p.: 1409/1989, Beirut: Lebanon, Vol. 4, p. 351.

Worship and Its Fruits

The goal of the chapter is to explain the concept of worship in the noble *sunnah* and the verses of the Noble Qur'ān and highlight its effect on man's worldly life and relationship to God ﷻ through understanding the following:

1. The worship of God in Qur'ānic verses and the narrations.

2. Worship is not limited to rituals.

3. The fruits of worship.

From the noble Prophet ﷺ: "The best of people is he who loves (*'ashiqa*) worship that he embraces it and adores it with his heart, proceeds with it with his body, and dedicates himself to it. Such a person does not care whether he woke up to hardship or ease."[23]

The Worship of God in the Verses and Narrations

In many of its verses, the Noble Qur'ān called for proper worship and prohibited deviated worship.

---

[23] Kulaynī, Shaykh Muḥammad b. Yaʿqūb, *al-Kāfī*, ed. and corr. ʿAlī Akbar al-Ghaffārī, Tehran: Dār al-Kutub al-Islāmiyya, 1363 SH, 5th ed., Vol. 2, p. 83.

The Holy Book mentioned that the purpose of creation is worship, and it mentioned some of the effects of worship on man. We will include some of these verses here.

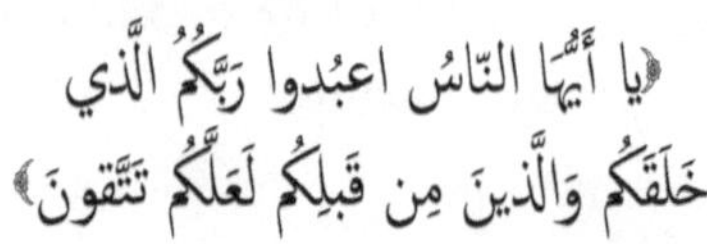

{yā-'ayyuhā n-nāsu 'budū rabbakumu lladhī khalaqakum wa-lladhīna min qablikum la'allakum tattaqūna}

{O mankind! Worship your Lord, who created you and those who were before you, so that you may be Godwary}[24]

This noble verse calls on humankind to worship the Creator ﷻ. In other verses, we find a prohibition against worshiping Satan:

---

[24] Sūrat al-Baqarah, Verse 21.

*❲’a-lam ’a‘had ’ilaykum yā-banī ’ādama ’an lā
ta‘budū sh-shayṭāna ’innahū lakum ‘aduwwun
mubīnᵘⁿ❳*

﴿وَأَنِ اعبُدونِي ۚ هٰذا صِراطٌ مُستَقيمٌ﴾

❲wa-’ani ‘budūnī hādhā ṣirāṭun mustaqīmᵘⁿ❳

﴿وَلَقَد أَضَلَّ مِنكُم جِبِلًّا كَثيرًا ۖ أَفَلَم تَكونوا تَعقِلونَ﴾

*❲wa-la-qad ’aḍalla minkum jibillan kathīran ’a-fa-
lam takūnū ta‘qilūnᵃ❳*

*❲'Did I not exhort you, O children of Adam, saying,
"Do not worship Satan. He is indeed your manifest
enemy. Worship Me. That is a straight path!"
Certainly he has led astray many of your
generations. Did you not use to apply reason?❳[25]*

There is also a command to be sincere in worship:

﴿قُل إِنّي أُمِرتُ أَن أَعبُدَ اللَّهَ مُخلِصًا لَهُ الدّينَ﴾

*❲qul ’innī ’umirtu ’an ’a‘buda llāha mukhliṣan
lahu d-dīnᵃ❳*

---

[25] Sūrat Yā Sīn, Verses 61-63.

❨Say, 'Indeed I have been commanded to worship God with exclusive faith in Him❩[26]

Elsewhere, a verse calls on the believers to declare that they are firm about worshiping God ﷻ and abandoning worshiping everything other than Him:

﴿قُل يا أَيُّها الكافِرونَ﴾

❨qul yā-'ayyuhā l-kāfirūnᵃ❩

﴿لا أَعبُدُ ما تَعبُدونَ﴾

❨lā 'a'budu mā ta'budūnᵃ❩

﴿وَلا أَنتُم عابِدونَ ما أَعبُدُ﴾

❨wa-lā 'antum 'ābidūna mā 'a'budᵘ❩

❨Say, 'O faithless ones! I do not worship what you worship, nor do you worship what I worship❩[27]

---

[26] Sūrat al-Zumar, Verse 11.

[27] Sūrat al-Kāfirūn, Verses 1-2.

As for the domain of ḥadīth, it specifies worship in a comprehensive manner, mentioning the purpose of worship, the kinds of worshipers, and the definition of the true worshiper. In other words, the ḥadīths did not limit the concept of worship to the acts of worship that people are familiar with. The narrations on the topic include the following. Imām 'Alī al-Riḍā ﷺ was asked about the reason for worship, and he said, "... so that they do not forget to remember Him, abandon His etiquette, or become distracted from His commands and prohibitions which lead to their righteousness and upright. They would become heedless and hard-hearted if left to themselves without worship."[28] Imām Ja'far al-Ṣādiq ﷺ says, "Worship is not in bowing and prostrating. It is obeying other men. Whoever obeys the created about disobeying the Creator has worshiped him."[29]

Worship Is Not Limited to Rituals

In truth, worship is a noun that includes all the sayings and the manifest and concealed deeds that

---

[28] 'Majlisī, 'Allamah Muḥammad Bāqir, *Biḥār al-Anwār*, Vol. 6, p. 63.

[29] Majlisī, 'Allamah Muḥammad Bāqir, *Biḥār al-Anwār*, Vol. 68, p. 116.

God ﷻ loves and is pleased by. Worship involves absolute humility before God ﷻ while loving Him. This comprehensive meaning of worship in Islam lies behind the message of all messengers and is a constant of their messages throughout history. A prophet did not command his people to worship God ﷻ. God ﷻ said,

$$\text{﴿وَما أَرسَلنا مِن قَبلِكَ مِن رَسولٍ إِلّا نوحي إِلَيهِ أَنَّهُ لا إِلٰهَ إِلّا أَنا فَاعبُدونِ﴾}$$

⟨*wa-mā ʾarsalnā min qablika min rasūlin ʾillā nūḥī ʾilayhi ʾannahū lā ʾilāha ʾillā ʾana fa-ʿbudūni*⟩

⟨*We did not send any apostle before you but We revealed to him that 'There is no god except Me; so worship Me.'*⟩[30]

Worshiping God ﷻ is not limited to rituals and practices related to a person's life as an independent individual; it includes individual life and life in society. Worship is organized based on the individual's relationships to God ﷻ, the soul, other people, and the universe. Every good deed done for the sake of God ﷻ is an act of worship, regardless of whether it is an individual or a communal act.

---

[30] Sūrat al-Anbiyāʾ, Verse 25.

Prayer, almsgiving (*ṣadaqa*), jihād, contemplating God's creation, helping the weak, making the corrupt righteous, being trustworthy (*adā' al-amāna*), being, refusing injustice, not drinking alcohol, boycotting usury (*ribā*) and acts of monopoly (*iḥtikār*) are all kinds of worship. This is as long as the motivation behind doing or avoiding those things complies with God's ﷻ command.

The Fruits of Worship

Because Islam is a comprehensive religion that takes into consideration worship in Islam has effects and benefits on the individual and social level. Among the fruits of worship are the following.

1. It enriches the heart. From Imām al-Ṣādiq ﷺ: "It is written in the Torah: 'O son of Adam, dedicate yourself to worshiping Me, and I will enrich your heart without abandoning you to that which you seek. It would be incumbent on me to satisfy your need and fill your heart with fear of Me. If you do not dedicate yourself to My worship, I will fill your heart with worldly things that occupy you, and then I will not

satisfy your need, but rather I will abandon to that which you are seeking."[31]

2. It leads to blessing in the Hereafter. From Imām al-Ṣādiq ﷺ: "God said, 'O My sincere servants, enjoy worshiping Me in this world, for you will be blessed by it in the Hereafter."[32]

3. It makes God boast about the worshiper to the angels. From the noble Prophet ﷺ: "God boasts about a young worshiper to the angels. He says, 'Look at My servant. He has abandoned his desire for My sake."[33]

4. God will make the worshiper vanquish Satan. From Imām al-Ṣādiq ﷺ, from his forefathers ﷺ: "The Prophet said to his companions, 'Would you like me to tell you about something that causes Satan to be as far away from you as the East is from the West?' They said, "Yes.' He said, 'Fasting blackens Satan's face, almsgiving breaks his back, loving each

---

[31] Kulaynī, Shaykh Muḥammad b. Yaʻqūb, *al-Kāfī*, Vol. 2, p. 83.

[32] Ibid.

[33] al-Hindī, ʻAlī al-Muttaqī, *Kanz al-ʻUmmāl fī Sunan al-Aqwāl wal-Afʻāl*, Vol. 15, p. 776.

other for God's sake and helping each other to do good deeds ends him, and seeking forgiveness (*istighfār*) slices his jugular vein. Furthermore, everything has a *zakāt*, and the *zakāt* of bodies is fasting."[34]

5.   The worshiper is admitted into Paradise: From Imām al-Ṣādiq ﷺ: "God will admit three categories of people into Paradise without reckoning: a just leader, a truthful servant, and an old man who has spent his life in worshiping God."[35]

---

[34] Majlisī, ʿAllamah Muḥammad Bāqir, *Biḥār al-Anwār*, Vol. 66, p. 380.

[35] Ibid., Vol. 26, p. 261.

Heedlessness (al-Ghaflah)

The goal of the chapter is to highlight the disadvantages of heedlessness (*al-Ghaflah*), its causes, and its adverse effects on man through understanding the following:

1. The disadvantages of heedlessness.

2. The causes of heedlessness.

3. Heedlessness and hard-heartedness.

Imām Muḥammad al-Bāqir ﷸ, "Never be heedless, for heedlessness leads to hard-heartedness."[36]

The Disadvantages of Heedlessness

God ﷻ said,

﴿وَلَقَد ذَرَأنا لِجَهَنَّمَ كَثيرًا مِنَ الجِنِّ وَالإِنسِ ۖ لَهُم قُلوبٌ لا يَفقَهونَ بِها وَلَهُم أَعيُنٌ لا يُبصِرونَ بِها وَلَهُم آذانٌ لا يَسمَعونَ بِها ۚ أُولٰئِكَ كَالأَنعامِ بَل هُم أَضَلُّ ۚ أُولٰئِكَ هُمُ الغافِلونَ﴾

*⟨wa-la-qad dhara'nā li-jahannama kathīran mina
l-jinni wa-l-'insi lahum qulūbun lā yafqahūna bihā
wa-lahum 'a'yunun lā yubṣirūna bihā wa-lahum*

---

36 Majlisī, ʿAllamah Muḥammad Bāqir, *Biḥār al-Anwār*, Vol. 74, p. 164.

'ādhānun lā yasma'ūna bihā 'ulā'ika ka-l-'an'āmi
bal hum 'aḍallu 'ulā'ika humu l-ghāfilūnᵃ⟩

⟨*Certainly We have created for hell many of the jinn
and humans: they have hearts with which they do
not understand, they have eyes with which they do
not see, they have ears with which they do not hear.
They are like cattle; rather they are more astray. It is
they who are the heedless*⟩[37]

Being heedless of God ﷻ increasingly tarnishes the
heart, enables the soul and Satan to conquer man,
and increases corruption. In contrast, mentioning
God ﷻ and remembering Him polish the heart,
make it pure, and turn it into a mirror for the
Beloved. They also purify the spirit and rid man of
the shackles of the soul.[38]

Heedlessness is an excellent reason for the deviation
and turning away from guidance. God ﷻ said,

---

[37] Sūrat al-Aʿrāf, Verse 179.

  Cf. 8:21-24; 8:55; 25:44.

[38] Khumaynī, Sayyid Rūḥullāh Mūsawī, *al-Kalimāt al-Qiṣār:
Mawāʿiz wa-Hikam min Kalām al-Imām al-Khumaynī*,
Beirut: Dār al-Wasīla, 1416/1995, 1ˢᵗ ed., p. 15.

﴿سَأَصْرِفُ عَنْ آيَاتِيَ الَّذِينَ يَتَكَبَّرُونَ فِي الْأَرْضِ بِغَيْرِ الْحَقِّ وَإِن يَرَوْا كُلَّ آيَةٍ لَا يُؤْمِنُوا بِهَا وَإِن يَرَوْا سَبِيلَ الرُّشْدِ لَا يَتَّخِذُوهُ سَبِيلًا وَإِن يَرَوْا سَبِيلَ الْغَيِّ يَتَّخِذُوهُ سَبِيلًا ۚ ذَٰلِكَ بِأَنَّهُمْ كَذَّبُوا بِآيَاتِنَا وَكَانُوا عَنْهَا غَافِلِينَ﴾

◖sa-ʾaṣrifu ʿan ʾāyātiya lladhīna yatakabbarūna fī l-ʾarḍi bi-ghayri l-ḥaqqi wa-ʾin yaraw kulla ʾāyatin lā yuʾminū bihā wa-ʾin yaraw sabīla r-rushdi lā yattakhidhūhu sabīlan wa-ʾin yaraw sabīla l-ghayyi yattakhidhūhu sabīlan dhālika bi-ʾannahum kadhdhabū bi-ʾāyātinā wa-kānū ʿanhā ghāfilīnᵃ◗

◖Soon I shall turn away from My signs those who are unduly arrogant in the earth: [even] though they should see every sign, they will not believe in it, and if they see the way of rectitude they will not take it as [their] way, and if they see the way of error they will take it as [their] way. That is because they deny Our signs and are oblivious to them.◗[39]

Heedlessness is also a reason for punishment and suffering a wrong end (*sūʾ al-khātima*). God ﷻ says He tried to make Pharaoh's clan remember through His signs, but they refused:

---

[39] Sūrat al-Aʿrāf, Verse 146.

﴿فَانتَقَمْنا مِنْهُم فَأَغْرَقْناهُم فِي الْيَمِّ بِأَنَّهُم كَذَّبوا بِآياتِنا وَكانوا عَنْها غافِلينَ﴾

﴿fa-ntaqamnā minhum fa-'aghraqnāhum fī l-yammi bi-'annahum kadhdhabū bi-'āyātinā wa-kānū 'anhā ghāfilīnᵃ﴾

﴿So We took vengeance on them and drowned them in the sea, for they denied Our signs and were oblivious to them﴾40

The Causes of Heedlessness

The most critical causes of heedlessness include:

1. Forgetting the purpose of creation. God ﷻ said,

﴿وَما خَلَقْتُ الْجِنَّ والإِنسَ إِلّا لِيَعْبُدونِ﴾

﴿wa-mā khalaqtu l-jinna wa-l-'insa 'illā li-ya'budūnⁱ﴾

﴿I did not create the jinn and the humans except that they may worship Me﴾41

---

40 Sūrat al-Aʿrāf, Verse 136.

41 Sūrat al-Dhāriyāt, Verse 56.

Our Lord ﷻ created us for a sublime purpose; He did not neglect us:

﴿أَفَحَسِبْتُمْ أَنَّمَا خَلَقْنَاكُمْ عَبَثًا وَأَنَّكُمْ إِلَيْنَا لَا تُرْجَعُونَ﴾

﴿'a-fa-ḥasibtum 'annamā khalaqnākum 'abathan wa-'annakum 'ilaynā lā turja'ūnᵃ﴾

﴿فَتَعَالَى اللَّهُ الْمَلِكُ الْحَقُّ ۗ لَا إِلَهَ إِلَّا هُوَ رَبُّ الْعَرْشِ الْكَرِيمِ﴾

﴿fa-ta'ālā llāhu l-maliku l-ḥaqqu lā 'ilāha 'illā huwa rabbu l-'arshi l-karīmⁱ﴾

﴿Did you suppose that We created you aimlessly, and that you will not be brought back to Us?' So exalted is God, the True Sovereign, there is no god except Him, the Lord of the Noble Throne﴾[42]

Whenever a person forgets the purpose behind his creation, he falls heedless.

2. Becoming lax about sins. The more a Muslim is lax about committing sins, the more heedlessness will take control of his heart. From the Prophet ﷺ: "Tribulations are presented to the hearts like mats are put on display, time and

____

[42] Sūrat al-Mu'minūn, Verses 115-116.

time again [or: so seek protection from them].[43] Any heart that absorbs these tribulations grows a black spot, and any heart that rejects them grows a white spot. Hearts are divided into two kinds: a grayish, deviant heart that does not know the right or refuse the wrong, except its whims; and a white heart that any tribulation cannot harm for as long as the heavens and the earth remains."[44]

Heedlessness and Hard-Heartedness

Heedlessness is on the other end of hasting and rushing to do good deeds. A heedless person even forgets his legal duty and becomes occupied with other things. God ﷻ said,

﴿قَالُوا بَلَىٰ وَلَٰكِنَّكُمْ فَتَنتُمْ أَنفُسَكُمْ وَتَرَبَّصْتُمْ وَارْتَبْتُمْ وَغَرَّتْكُمُ الْأَمَانِيُّ﴾

﴿qālū balā wa-lākinnakum fatantum ʾanfusakum wa-tarabbaṣtum wa-rtabtum wa-gharratkumu l-ʾamāniyyu﴾

---

43 Either *ʿiwadan ʿiwadan* or *ʿiwadhan ʿiwadhan*.

44 al-Māzandarānī, al-Mawlā Muḥammad Ṣāliḥ b. Aḥmad, *Sharḥ Uṣūl al-Kāfī*, comm. Mīrzā Abū al-Ḥasan al-Shaʿrānī, corr. Sayyid ʿAlī ʿĀshūr, Beirut: Dār Iḥyāʾ al-Turāth, 1421/2000, 1st ed., Vol. 12, p. 15.

⟨*They will say, 'Yes! But you cast yourselves into temptation, and you awaited* and were doubtful, and [false] hopes deceived you*⟩[45]

The hypocrites will ask the believers,

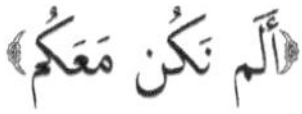

⟨*'a-lam nakun ma'akum*⟩

⟨*'Did we not use to be with you?'*⟩[46]

They mean to ask, "Were we not neighbors, attendees of the same mosque, and companions in jihād? What caused you to reach such heights of happiness while we remain in this absolute darkness?"

The believers respond,

---

[45] Sūrat al-Ḥadīd, Verse 14.

* That is, waited for a reverse of fortune for Muslims. See 4:41, 9:50-52, 9:98, 23:25, 52:30-31.

[46] Ibid.

❨*balā wa-lākinnakum fatantum ʾanfusakum*❩

❨*'Yes! But you cast yourselves into temptation*❩[47]

God ﷻ says in another verse:

﴿أَلَمْ يَأْنِ لِلَّذِينَ آمَنُوا أَن تَخْشَعَ قُلُوبُهُمْ لِذِكْرِ اللَّهِ وَما نَزَلَ مِنَ الْحَقِّ وَلا يَكُونُوا كَالَّذِينَ أُوتُوا الْكِتَابَ مِن قَبْلُ فَطالَ عَلَيْهِمُ الأَمَدُ فَقَسَت قُلُوبُهُمْ ۖ وَكَثِيرٌ مِنْهُم فاسِقُونَ﴾

❨*ʾa-lam yaʾni li-lladhīna ʾāmanū ʾan takhshaʿa qulūbuhum li-dhikri llāhi wa-mā nazala mina l-ḥaqqi wa-lā yakūnū ka-lladhīna ʾūtū l-kitāba min qablu fa-ṭāla ʿalayhimu l-ʾamadu fa-qasat qulūbuhum wa-kathīrun minhum fāsiqūnᵃ*❩

❨*Is it not time yet for those who have faith that their hearts should be humbled for God's remembrance and to the truth which has come down [to them], and to be not like those who were given the Book before?* Time took its toll on them and so their hearts*❩

---

were hardened, and many of them are transgressors[48]

Suppose the heart is deprived of God's ﷻ light of guidance and becomes occupied with the monotonous and mundane aspects of life through heedlessness. In that case, it will lose its tenderness and emotionality. Even sermons will no longer affect it. As a result, the heart will gradually forget its creation's initial purpose, destination, the goal behind sending the prophets ﷺ, and the establishment of the systems of Prophethood, Imāmate, and testimony. This forgetfulness and heedlessness make the heart as hard as a rock.

For this reason, Imām al-Bāqir ﷺ says, "Never be heedless, for heedlessness leads to hard-heartedness.[49] Be careful so you will not be tried heedlessly and carelessly, as they lead to hard-heartedness. Unfortunately, modern global culture tends to be like this by trying to forget sadness, sorrow, fear, and other negative emotions by not

---

[48] Sūrat al-Ḥadīd, Verse 16.

* That is, the Jews.

[49] Majlisī, 'Allamah Muḥammad Bāqir, *Biḥār al-Anwār*, Vol. 74, p. 164.

thinking about them. People would rather be careless. However, negligence and carelessness harden the heart so that the truth no longer affects it, no matter how often it hears it.[50]

---

[50] From a lecture by Āyatullāh Muḥammad Taqī Miṣbāḥ Yazdī, given at the office of Āyatullāh Sayyid ʿAlī Ḥusaynī Khāminaʾī in Qom on August 20, 2008.

Remembering and Preparing for Death

The goal of the chapter is to urge people to remember death, be prepared, and be on guard about it through understanding the following:

1. The effects of remembering death.

2. Being on guard for death.

3. Preparing for death.

4. The death of the believer.

5. The death of the people of Hell.

The Commander of the Believers ﷺ: "Remember death often, and remember what you are coming to and how you will end up after death. This way, death will come to you while you are prepared and on your guard for it, not in a sudden way that takes you aback. Never allow yourself to be cheated by how the people cling to it and fight over it like dogs. God already told you about this world, and the world told you about itself and revealed its faults to you."[51]

---

[51] Sharīf Raḍī, Muḥammad b. al-Ḥusayn, *Nahj al-Balāgha*, p. 400.

The Effects of Remembering Death

Death is the truth that is the destiny of every human being. In truth, death is transitioning from the abode of tribulation and testing to the abode of reward and recompense. Whoever did well will find the time of reward pleasant, and whoever committed evil deeds will fear it. Imām al-Ṣādiq ﷺ says, "A servant does not truly reach the level of true faith until death is dearer to him than life."[52]

Undoubtedly, remembering death affects a person's spirituality and conduct. When remembering death, people may be divided into two categories. The first category includes the people who are heedless of the Hereafter and are only concerned about their numbered days in this world. Their goals revolve around everyday needs. This kind of person views death as the end of hope, goals, and existence. For this reason, it is logical that remembering death would make them hopeless and depressed. For this reason, they often avoid the topic.

---

[52] Kulaynī, Shaykh Muḥammad b. Yaʻqūb, *al-Kāfī*, Vol. 8, p. 253.

The second category includes people who know God ﷻ and know there is a day for reckoning and reward. Their true goal does not stop at these numbered days in this life, nor are their ambitions limited to daily needs. Although they still remember their share of this world, their goal remains the Hereafter. They set the foundations for it and prepare to reach that stage in the best possible condition. For these people, remembering death has many benefits, including the following.

1. Death motivates them to work hard and be energetic to benefit from the world as much as possible as a groundwork for the Hereafter. Their window of opportunity is limited, after all.

2. It establishes the real goal, the Hereafter, more firmly in their souls. Death makes this goal ever-present, and it corrects a person's course.

3. Death helps control the urges of the soul and the desires. It cultivates these urges and places them in their proper context. From the Prophet ﷺ: "Remember death frequently, for it cleanses your sins and makes you abstemious about this world. If you mention death when you are rich, it will demolish your riches, and if

you mention it when you are poor, it will make you satisfied with your lot."[53]

Being On Guard for Death

"This way, death will come to you while you are on your guard for it...."

Man's trouble lies in the multiple veils over his heart, which prevent him from remembering God ﷻ and cause him to grow distant from Him. Remembering death is a helpful factor that causes these veils to be lifted. The Prophet ﷺ said, "Just like iron, hearts become covered with rust." Someone asked, "How may they be polished?" He ﷺ said, "By reciting the Qur'ān and remembering death."[54]

How does remembering death contribute to lifting these veils? This happens when a person senses that his life will be no more. Imām 'Alī ؏ says, "Death is the destroyer of your pleasures, the ruiner of your desires, and the thing that separates you from your

---

[53] al-Hindī, 'Alī al-Muttaqī, *Kanz al-'Ummāl fī Sunan al-Aqwāl wal-Af'āl*, Vol. 15, p. 543.

[54] al-Aḥsā'ī, Ibn Abī Jumhūr, *'Awālī al-La'ālī al-'Azīziyya fil-Aḥādīth al-Dīniyya*, Vol. 1, p. 280.

goals. It is an unwelcome visitor, but it is a worthy opponent that cannot be beaten and a killer that cannot be brought to justice. Its ropes have ensnared you ... and its deep darknesses and imminent troubles will soon be upon you."[55]

Some people deal with death as if it was an uncertain thing. The Commander of the Believers ﷺ referred to this when he said, "I have never seen anything more like certain belief to human beings than doubt. Every day, he bids people farewell to their graves and walks in their funerals, yet he returns to the vanity of this world and does not refrain from desires and sins. Even if this poor son of Adam did not have sins lying in wait and a reckoning to come, and the only thing in store was a death that would scatter his relations and disperses his people and orphan his children, he should be on his guard of death to the utmost."[56] Can any person hope for eternal life in this world? A narration from the Commander of Believers ﷺ states, "If anyone were to find a ladder that leads to eternal life or a way to keep death away, it would

---

[55] Sharīf Raḍī, Muḥammad b. al-Ḥusayn, *Nahj al-Balāgha*, p. 351.

[56] Majlisī, ʿAllamah Muḥammad Bāqir, *Biḥār al-Anwār*, Vol. 6, p. 137.

have been Sulaymān b. Dawūd ﷺ. God gave him control over the kingdom of the Jinn and humankind, prophethood, and great nearness to Him. However, when he got the last portion and spent the last of his lifetime, the bows of mortality struck him with the arrows of death. His home became empty, his residences were neglected, and others inherited them."[57]

Preparing for Death

"While you are prepared [...] for it."

Anyone who sets out to travel prepares for him for it at the level of ability and strength in a way that enables him to reach his destination. Man is like this: he must prepare in this world in a way that is helpful to him in the Hereafter.

From Imām ʿAlī ﷺ: "O servants of God, be on your guard against death and how near it is, and prepare for it. It will bring you a great and magnificent thing: goodness without evil or evil without goodness."[58]

---

[57] Sharīf Raḍī, Muḥammad b. al-Ḥusayn, *Nahj al-Balāgha*, p. 263.

[58] Ibid., p. 384.

"Not in a sudden way that takes you aback."

The narrations mention the manner of the believer and the unbeliever's death. God ﷻ says,

﴿قَدْ خَسِرَ الَّذِينَ كَذَّبُوا بِلِقَاءِ اللَّهِ ۖ حَتَّىٰ إِذَا جَاءَتْهُمُ السَّاعَةُ بَغْتَةً قَالُوا يَا حَسْرَتَنَا عَلَىٰ مَا فَرَّطْنَا فِيهَا وَهُمْ يَحْمِلُونَ أَوْزَارَهُمْ عَلَىٰ ظُهُورِهِمْ ۚ أَلَا سَاءَ مَا يَزِرُونَ﴾

qad khasira lladhīna kadhdhabū bi-liqā'i llāhi ḥattā 'idhā jā'athumu s-sā'atu baghtatan qālū yā-ḥasratanā 'alā mā farraṭnā fīhā wa-hum yaḥmilūna 'awzārahum 'alā ẓuhūrihim 'a-lā sā'a mā yazirūn[a]

⟨They are certainly losers who deny the encounter with God. When the Hour overtakes them suddenly, they will say, 'Alas for us, for what we neglected in it!' And they will bear their burdens on their backs. Look! Evil is what they bear!⟩[59]

The Death of the Believer

1. The angel of death: The Prophet ﷺ said, "The angel of death stands before the believer at his

---

death like a humble slave stands before his master. The angel of death and his retinue do not approach the believer before saluting him and giving him tidings of Paradise."[60]

2. The departure of the spirit (*khurūj al-rūḥ*): From the Prophet ﷺ: "Those of our Shīʿa who love us the most find the departure of the soul like drinking cold water that quenches the heart on a summer day. The rest of our Shīʿa die as if they are going to sleep; they could not be happier about their death."[61]

3. Good tidings: From the Prophet ﷺ: "The first tidings given to the believer are ease, abundance, and a garden of bliss.[62] The first tidings given to the believer are when he is told, 'O friend of God, rejoice in God's pleasure and Paradise! You have reached the best destination. God forgave those who walked in your funeral,

---

[60] Ṣadūq, Shaykh Muḥammad b. ʿAlī, *Man Lā Yaḥḍuruh al-Faqīh*, corr. And comm. ʿAlī Akbar al-Ghaffārī, Qom: Muʾassasat al-Nashr al-Islāmī al-Tābiʿa li-Jamāʿat al-Mudarrisīn, 1414 AH, 2nd ed., Vol. 1, p. 135.

[61] Majlisī, ʿAllamah Muḥammad Bāqir, *Biḥār al-Anwār*, Vol. 6, p. 162.

[62] Translator's note: see Sūrat al-Wāqiʿa, Verse 89.

answered those who asked for forgiveness, and accepted their testimonies on your behalf."[63]

The Death of the People of Hell

Their death is as follows.

1. The angel of death:

﴿وَلَو تَرَىٰ إذ يَتَوَفَّ الَّذينَ كَفَرُوا ۙ المَلَائِكَةُ يَضرِبونَ وُجوهَهُم وَأَدبارَهُم وَذوقوا عَذابَ الحَريقِ﴾

❨wa-law tarā ʾidh yatawaffā lladhīna kafarū l-malāʾikatu yaḍribūna wujūhahum wa-ʾadbārahum wa-dhūqū ʿadhāba l-ḥarīqi❩

❨*Were you to see when the angels take away the faithless, striking their faces and their backs, [saying], 'Taste the punishment of the burning*❩[64]

2. From Imām al-Bāqir ﷺ: "He [the angel of death] comes to the unbeliever with a detestable and scowling face. His eyes are like

---

[63] al-Hindī, ʿAlī al-Muttaqī, *Kanz al-ʿUmmāl fī Sunan al-Aqwāl wal-Afʿāl*, Vol. 15, p. 596.

[64] Sūrat al-Anfāl, Verse 50.

swift lightning, and his voice is booming thunder. His color is like the pitch black night, and his breath is like flames of fire. His head is at the level of the sky of this world, and he has one foot in the East, and one foot in the West, and both of his legs are in the air."[65]

3. An evil ending: God ﷻ says,

﴿وَلَو تَرىٰ إِذِ الظّالِمونَ في غَمَراتِ المَوتِ وَالمَلائِكَةُ باسِطو أَيديهِم أَخرِجوا أَنفُسَكُمُ اليَومَ تُجزَونَ عَذابَ الهونِ بِما كُنتُم تَقولونَ عَلَى اللَّهِ غَيرَ الحَقِّ وَكُنتُم عَن آياتِهِ تَستَكبِرونَ﴾

⟨wa-law tarā ʾidhi ẓ-ẓālimūna fī ghamarāti l-mawti wa-l-malāʾikatu bāsiṭū ʾaydīhim ʾakhrijū ʾanfusakumu l-yawma tujzawna ʿadhāba l-hūni bi-mā kuntum taqūlūna ʿalā llāhi ghayra l-ḥaqqi wa-kuntum ʿan ʾāyātihī tastakbirūnᵃ⟩

⟨*Were you to see when the wrongdoers are in the throes of death, and the angels extend their hands [saying]: 'Give up your souls! Today you shall be requited with a humiliating punishment because of*

---

⁶⁵ Mufīd, Shaykh Muḥammad, *al-Ikhtiṣāṣ*, ed. ʿAlī Akbar al-Ghaffārī and Sayyid Maḥmūd al-Zarandī, Beirut: Dār al-Mufīd lil-Ṭibāʿa wal-Nashr, 1414/1993, 2nd ed., p. 359.

what you used to attribute to God untruly, and for your being disdainful towards His signs.[66]

---

[66] Sūrat al-Anʿām, Verse 93.

Delegating Matters to God and Reassurance

The goal of the chapter is to explain the meaning of delegating matters to God (*al-tafwīḍ*) and its effects on the mind and soul through understanding the following:

1. The meaning of the entire delegation.

2. The only independent source of influence is God.

3. Examples of divine blessings given to the pious (*al-muttaqīn*)

Imām al-Bāqir ﷺ: "Arrive to the true rest of the soul through sound delegation to God, seek bodily rest by giving the heart rest, and the true rest of the heart through making as few mistakes as possible."[67]

The Meaning of Real Delegation

The Imām's ﷺ saying, "Arrive sincerely to the soul's rest through sound delegation," means that if you want to be wholly reassured and free of worry,

---

[67] Majlisī, ʿAllamah Muḥammad Bāqir, *Biḥār al-Anwār*, Vol. 75, p. 164.

delegate your affairs to God. He ﷻ did not say, "Arrive sincerely to the soul's rest through delegation, but through "sound delegation" (*siḥḥat al-tafwīḍ*). Perhaps, Imām al-Bāqir ﷺ wanted to alert us that sometimes a person deceives himself and does not truly delegate his affairs to God ﷻ. This person would merely say, "I have delegated the affair to God," out of laziness. This is not proper delegation; it is lazy and impolite [to God]. Proper delegation is in being able to do something and doing it out of religious obligation while relying on God ﷻ. Such a person does not care whether the outcome of his action was success or failure.[68]

The Only Independent Source of Influence Is God ﷻ

We initially understand the system of cause and effect to be independent in its influence. For example, we think that the water we drink quenches our thirst, regardless of whether there is a God, but this is false. All divine religions, prophets, and messengers came to tell us that what we see with our eyes is the surface layer of this life and that

---

[68] From a lecture by Āyatullāh Muḥammad Taqī Miṣbāḥ Yazdī, given at the office of Āyatullāh Sayyid ʿAlī Ḥusaynī Khāminaʾī in Qom on August 15, 2008.

this life has an inner dimension and a loftier truth than shallow things.

﴿يَا أَيُّهَا النَّاسُ اتَّقُوا رَبَّكُمْ وَاخْشَوْا يَوْمًا لَا يَجْزِي وَالِدٌ عَن وَلَدِهِ وَلَا مَوْلُودٌ هُوَ جَازٍ عَن وَالِدِهِ شَيْئًا إِنَّ وَعْدَ اللَّهِ حَقٌّ فَلَا تَغُرَّنَّكُمُ الْحَيَاةُ الدُّنْيَا وَلَا يَغُرَّنَّكُم بِاللَّهِ الْغَرُورُ﴾

⟨yā-'ayyuhā n-nāsu ttaqū rabbakum wa-khshaw
yawman lā yajzī wālidun 'an waladihī wa-lā
mawlūdun huwa jāzin 'an wālidihī shay'an 'inna
wa'da llāhi ḥaqqun fa-lā taghurrannakumu l-
ḥayātu d-dunyā wa-lā yaghurrannakum bi-llāhi l-
gharūr"⟩

⟨O mankind! Be wary of your Lord and fear the day
when a father shall not atone for his child, nor the
child shall atone for its father in any wise. Indeed
God's promise is true. So do not let the life of the
world deceive you, nor let the Deceiver deceive you*
concerning God⟩[69]

Do not let this life cheat you!

––––––––––––––––––

[69] Surat Luqmān, Verse 33.

* That is, Satan, or anything that diverts a human being from the path of God.

Examples of Divine Blessings Given To the Pious

1. Loving faith: Some people do not use this divine design that's bursting with countless divine blessings except through the system of the Sharī'a. God ﷻ gives such people other blessings that are not like material bounties, which include a heart full of light, finding comfort in God, having one's spiritual eyes opened, witnessing the truths, and so on. God ﷻ said,

﴿فَمَن يُرِدِ اللَّهُ أَن يَهْدِيَهُ يَشْرَحْ صَدْرَهُ لِلْإِسْلامِ ۖ وَمَن يُرِدْ أَن يُضِلَّهُ يَجْعَلْ صَدْرَهُ ضَيِّقًا حَرَجًا كَأَنَّمَا يَصَّعَّدُ فِي السَّمَاءِ ۚ كَذَٰلِكَ يَجْعَلُ اللَّهُ الرِّجْسَ عَلَى الَّذِينَ لا يُؤْمِنونَ﴾

﴿*fa-man yuridi llāhu 'an yahdiyahū yashraḥ ṣadrahū li-l-'islāmi wa-man yurid 'an yuḍillahū yaj'al ṣadrahū ḍayyiqan ḥarajan ka-'annamā yaṣṣa''adu fī s-samā'i ka-dhālika yaj'alu llāhu r-rijsa 'alā lladhīna lā yu'minūn*[a]﴾

﴿*Whomever God desires to guide, He opens his breast to Islam, and whomever He desires to lead astray, He makes his breast narrow and straitened as if he were climbing to a height.* Thus does God lay

*[spiritual] defilement on those who do not have
faith*❯70

In addition to material blessings common to
believers and unbelievers, God created other
blessings with which he favors those who use
material blessings correctly. God ﷻ says,

﴿يَا أَيُّهَا الَّذِينَ آمَنُوا اتَّقُوا اللَّهَ وَآمِنُوا بِرَسُولِهِ يُؤْتِكُمْ كِفْلَيْنِ مِن
رَحْمَتِهِ وَيَجْعَل لَّكُمْ نُورًا تَمْشُونَ بِهِ وَيَغْفِرْ لَكُمْ ۚ وَاللَّهُ غَفُورٌ رَحِيمٌ﴾

❮*yā-'ayyuhā lladhīna 'āmanū ttaqū llāha wa-
'āminū bi-rasūlihī yu'tikum kiflayni min
raḥmatihī wa-yaj'al lakum nūran tamshūna bihī
wa-yaghfir lakum wa-llāhu ghafūrun raḥīm^{un}*❯

❮*O you who have faith! Be wary of God and have
faith in His Apostle. He will grant you a double
share* (kiflayn) *of His mercy and give you a light to
walk by, and forgive you, and God is Forgiving,
Merciful*❯71

---

70 Sūrat al-An'ām, Verse 125.

*   That is, makes his spiritual and intellectual capacities
shrink.

71 Sūrat al-Ḥadīd, Verse 28.

The word *"kiflayn"* means two shares. Among the great blessings that God ﷻ favors His pious worshipers with is the blessing of loving faith and detesting faithlessness.

2. Divine sustenance (*rizq*): If a person uses God's ﷻ blessings, God will favor Him with another grace. God will make it easy for this person to benefit from worldly blessings. The Qur'ān says,

$$\text{﴿وَمَن يَتَّقِ اللَّهَ يَجْعَل لَّهُ مَخْرَجًا﴾}$$

﴾wa-man yattaqi llāha yaj'al lahū makhrajaⁿ﴿

$$\text{﴿وَيَرْزُقْهُ مِن حَيْثُ لَا يَحْتَسِبُ﴾}$$

﴾wa-yarzuqhu min ḥaythu lā yaḥtasibu﴿

﴾And whoever is wary of God, He shall make a way out for him (of the adversities of the world and the Hereafter) and provide for him from whence he does not reckon﴿[72]

3. God ﷻ does not leave the faithful to a dead end. This also applies to society, as He ﷻ says,

---

[72] Sūrat al-Ṭalāq, Verses 2-3.

$$\lang وَلَوْ أَنَّ أَهْلَ الْقُرَىٰ آمَنُوا وَاتَّقَوْا لَفَتَحْنَا عَلَيْهِم بَرَكَاتٍ مِنَ السَّمَاءِ وَالْأَرْضِ \rang$$

⟨wa-law 'anna 'ahla l-qurā 'āmanū wa-ttaqaw la-fataḥnā ʿalayhim barakātin mina s-samā'i wa-l-'arḍi⟩

⟨If the people of the towns had been faithful and Godwary, We would have opened to them blessings from the heaven and the earth⟩[73]

When the members of society are pious, keep the rulings of Islam in mind, and treat them as they are due, God will send down blessings upon them. In other words, He will give them access to divine blessings in a much more comfortable and abundant way.[74]

Comfort and Blessing

God ﷻ has another way of dealing with the faithful; He manages their affairs based on this relationship in a way that allows the pious person

---

[73] Sūrat al-Aʿrāf, Verse 96.

[74] From a lecture by Āyatullāh Muḥammad Taqī Miṣbāḥ Yazdī, given at the office of Āyatullāh Sayyid ʿAlī Ḥusaynī Khāmina'ī in Qom on August 15, 2008.

to spend his time on the best deeds. When the believer seeks lawful sustenance, that is a form of worship. However, there is a big difference between this kind of worship and pure worship, which revolves around nothing except the relationship with God ﷻ. When God ﷻ sees that His servant truly loves worship and wants to find comfort in Him and not get distracted by any other, He ﷻ will manage this servant's affairs so that he does not spend too much time on the affairs of this world. Such a person is acting on his religious obligation (*taklīf shar'ī*), which is striving to earn a living. He would, for example, open up shop and buy and sell, but all this is not an obstacle in the face of his worship. His affairs are managed beyond man's reason (*'aql*) alone. The supplication on the Day of 'Arafa (*du'ā' 'Arafa*) contains the following words: "My God, spare me of managing my affairs by managing my affairs Yourself, and spare me from choosing by choosing for me."[75]

---

[75] Majlisī, 'Allamah Muḥammad Bāqir, *Biḥār al-Anwār*, Vol. 95, p. 226.

Stopping Distractions

From Imām al-Bāqir ﷺ: "Arrive to [...] the true rest of the heart through making as few mistakes as possible." His ﷺ saying "making as few mistakes as possible" means "being as least disobedient as possible." In other words, if you would like to have a presence of mind and be able to focus, strive to lessen your acts of disobedience. We have religiously lawful and sensible ways of meeting our needs. However, if a person deviates from the correct path, he will face many detours and ups and downs. For example, there is a natural solution for fulfilling sexual instincts, which is marriage. However, when a person deviates from the correct path, he will seek other ways of satisfying this instinct. One unlawful look may occupy the mind for the rest of the day, making the person neglect his prayers and the rest of his religious deeds. Using the eyes, tongue, and ears haphazardly leads to distraction and a lack of energy, which may be harmful. This is why Imām al-Bāqir ﷺ told us that if we want to relieve our bodies, we should seek to have focus and presence of mind, and if we want to have focus and presence of mind, we should try to make as few mistakes as possible.[76]

---

[76] From a lecture by Āyatullāh Muḥammad Taqī Miṣbāḥ Yazdī, given at the office of Āyatullāh Sayyid ʿAlī Ḥusaynī Khāminaʾī in Qom on August 15, 2008.

Abstinence (zuhd) and Not Putting Too Much Stock in This World

The goal of the chapter is to explain abstinence's true meaning and merit (*zuhd*) and the necessity of not putting too much stock in this worldly life (*qiṣr al-amal*) through understanding the following:

1. The true meaning and value of abstinence

2. The sweetness of abstinence

3. The meaning of putting too much stock in this world (*ṭūl al-amal*)

4. Abstinence and not putting too much stock in this world

Imām al-Bāqir ﷺ: "And bring about the sweetness of abstinence by not putting too much stock in this world."[77]

---

[77] Majlisī, ʿAllamah Muḥammad Bāqir, *Biḥār al-Anwār*, Vol. 75, p. 164.

The True Meaning and Value of Abstinence

Abstinence in this world is a lofty station (*maqām*) of the worshipers of God ﷻ who are wayfarers (*sālikūn*) on the way to God. From the noble Prophet ﷺ: "God is not worshiped with anything better than through being abstinent towards this world."[78] The true meaning of abstinence is turning away from something in favor of something even better. This turning away and renouncement should be directed at something desired for it to be called abstinence. A genuine abstinent person finds constant comfort (*uns*) in God ﷻ, and obedience is his most prominent trait.

A genuine abstinent person does not feel happy about something coming his way, nor does he become sad over something he loses. The Commander of the Believers ؑ says, "All of abstinence lies in a few words in the Qur'ān. God said, 'So that you may not grieve for what escapes you, nor boast for what comes your way.' Whoever

---

[78] al-Mīrzā al-Nūrī, *Mustadrak al-Wasā'il wa-Mustanbaṭ al-Masā'il*, Beirut: Mu'assasat Āl al-Bayt li-Iḥyā' al-Turāth, 1408/1987, 1ˢᵗ ed., Vol. 12, p. 50.

does not grieve the past or boast about the future has abstinence covered on both fronts."[79]

The Sweetness of Abstinence

Why would abstinent people subject themselves to this hardship and trouble when the world is freely available to the pious (*al-barr*) and the profligate (*al-fājir*)? Imām al-Bāqir ﷺ revealed one of the secrets of abstinence and abstinent people, and he summarized it in four words: "the sweetness of abstinence." Abstinence has a sweetness that is familiar to good, virtuous, abstinent people who have pleased God ﷻ. Not putting too much stock in this world may bring this sweetness.

What Does Putting Too Much Stock In This World Mean?

Islamic ethics deeply frown upon putting too much stock in this world. From the Commander of the Faithful ﷺ: "I fear two things for you the most: following your desires and putting too much

---

[79] Ibn Abī al-Ḥadīd, ʿAbd al-Ḥamīd Hibatullāh, *Sharḥ Nahj al-Balāgha*, ed. Muḥammad Abū al-Faḍl Ibrāhīm, Qom: Maktabat Āyatullah al-Marʿashī al-Najafī, 1st ed., 1404 AH, Vol. 20, p. 87.

stock in this world."[80] This means that he ﷺ fears the Muslims because of two things. The first is obeying the desires and whims of the soul. However, it should be noted that not everything that the heart desires is bad and prohibited. The heart may also be inclined to something required in the Sharī'a. The concept of desire used in Islamic ethics contradicts religious law and reason (*al-'aql*). It refers to when the heart is inclined to what the soul desires, not what brings God's ﷻ love and pleasure. That is a dangerous thing. The second thing that the Imām ﷺ mentioned was putting too much stock in this world. He ﷺ is an expert on the illnesses of the soul and knows what may ruin this world and the next.

The Meaning of Putting Too Much Stock in This World

Hope, linguistically, means expectation. It is not a bad thing in itself. Without it, nothing could be achieved in human life. However, hope in the ethical Islamic context means wishful thinking that keeps a person from doing his religious obligations and other meaningful deeds. Aspirations that urge

---

[80] Majlisī, 'Allamah Muḥammad Bāqir, *Biḥār al-Anwār*, Vol. 74, p. 420.

a person toward perfection and the degree of nearness to God ﷻ are not like aspirations of becoming the wealthiest person in the world or a well-known and famous athlete. Wishful thinking is a stumbling block to fulfilling religious duties, so it is frowned upon.

From the Islamic ethics and cultural perspective, hopes and aspirations that make a person reach the degrees of perfection and closeness to God ﷻ are classified as high resolve (*'uluww al-himma*). It is not a wrong kind of hope to aspiring to higher ranks of piety, knowledge, industry, and management to serve one's people and *umma*, nor is it wrong to have a lot of money to help the poor. The condition has a reasonable way to achieve those hopes and aspirations.[81]

Abstinence and Not Putting Too Much Stock in This World

Not putting too much stock in this world and keeping death in mind makes a person abstinent and makes the world low in his eyes. After this,

---

[81] From a lecture by Āyatullāh Muḥammad Taqī Miṣbāḥ Yazdī, given at the office of Āyatullāh Sayyid 'Alī Ḥusaynī Khāmina'ī in Qom on August 15, 2008.

such a person pays the world no mind. From the Commander of the Faithful ﷺ: "May God have mercy on the person who does not put too much stock in this world, hastened to act before death, made good use of the time given him, and did as many good deeds as he could."[82]

Salmān said, "Three things make me laugh. A heedless person while God is not heedless of him, a seeker of this world while death seeks him, and someone who grins from ear to ear without knowing whether his Master ﷻ is pleased with him or angry at him."[83]

A man came into Abū Dharr al-Ghifārī's house and began observing it. He asked, "O Abū Dharr, where are your goods?" Abū Dharr said, "We have another house to which we are sending the best of our goods." The man told him, "You do need some goods as long as you are in this world," Abū Dharr said, "The owner of the house will not allow us to

---

[82] al-Laythī al-Wāsiṭī, Shaykh Kāfī al-Dīn ʿAlī b. Muḥammad, *ʿUyūn al-Ḥikam wal-Mawāʿiẓ*, p. 261.

[83] al-Barqī, Aḥmad b. Muḥammad b. Khālid, *al-Maḥāsin*, corr. and comm. Sayyid Jalāl al-Dīn al-Ḥusaynī, Tehran: Dār al-Kutub al-Islāmiyya, 1370 AH/1330 SH, Vol. 1, p. 4.

stay in it forever."[84] Abū Dharr was a stranger who walked alone, died alone, and will be resurrected alone. He is of Paradise (*huwa min al-janna*).

---

84 al-Bayhaqī, Aḥmad b. al-Ḥusayn, *Shuʿab al-Īmān*, Abū Hājar Muḥammad b. al-Saʿīd b. Basyūnī Zaghlūl, Beirut: Dār al-Kutub al-ʿIlmiyya, 1410/1990, 1st ed., Vol. 7, p. 378.

Despairing of God's Mercy

The goal of the chapter is to urge people not to despair and spreading hope through understanding the following:

1. Otherworldly despair (*al-ya's al-ukhrawī*)

2. The cure for otherworldly despair

3. Worldly despair

4. The cure for worldly despair

﴿قُل يا عِبادِيَ الَّذينَ أَسرَفوا عَلىٰ أَنفُسِهِم لا تَقنَطوا مِن رَحمَةِ اللَّهِ ۚ إِنَّ اللَّهَ يَغفِرُ الذُّنوبَ جَميعًا ۚ إِنَّهُ هُوَ الغَفورُ الرَّحيمُ﴾

﴿qul yā-ʿibādiya lladhīna ʾasrafū ʿalā ʾanfusihim lā taqnaṭū min raḥmati llāhi ʾinna llāha yaghfiru dh-dhunūba jamīʿan ʾinnahū huwa l-ghafūru r-raḥīmᵘ﴾

﴿Say [that God declares,] 'O My servants who have committed excesses against their own souls, do not despair of the mercy of God. Indeed God will forgive all sins. Indeed He is the Forgiving, the Merciful﴾[85]

The Varieties of Despair

One of the great sins is despairing of God's ﷻ mercy. This kind of despair is of two types.

Otherworldly Despair

This is when a person despairs God's ﷻ mercy and forgiveness. Many sinners think that the road to God ﷻ is closed off to them, especially when they commit grave sins (*al-kabā'ir*). They think that God ﷻ would not accept their repentance.

The Cure for Otherworldly Despair

Feeling guilty about bad deeds, especially if they are grave sins, completely occupies the mind of a person who wants to repent. This leads to despair. However, many things can cure otherworldly despair.

The Door to Repentance is Open

Repentance could be a decisive way of cutting ties with the past and starting a new life. It may even be like a rebirth of the person if it satisfies all the necessary conditions.

Imām al-Bāqir ؏: "Whoever repents of a sin is like someone who has not sinned at all, and whoever insists on a sin while repenting of it is like someone who is someone who is engaging in ridicule."[86]

Having Belief in Intercession

Having belief in intersession makes a person hope for pardon and forgiveness. This makes him reconsider the course of his life and encourages him to avoid the mistakes of the past. From Imām al-Bāqir ؏: "The believer intercedes for a neighbor who had not done even one good deed. The believer says, 'O Lord, what about my neighbor? He used to protect me from harm,' and his intercession is granted. God ﷻ says, 'I am your Lord, and I am the most worthy One to reward on your behalf.' God ﷻ then grants the neighbor entry into Paradise without a single good deed. The believer with the lowest level of intercession is allowed to intercede for thirty people."[87]

---

[86] Kulaynī, Shaykh Muḥammad b. Yaʿqūb, *al-Kāfī*, Vol. 2, p. 435.

[87] Ibid., Vol. 8, p. 101.

Caution: Between Hope and Fear

Despairing of God's ﷻ mercy indeed is one of the grave sins, but having false security (*amn*) about His ﷻ devising (*makr*) and punishment is also one of the grave sins. This calls for being cautious about both things: despair and false security.

The Noble Qur'ān considered fear and hope among the characteristics of the faithful; they are neither heedless about God's ﷻ wrath nor despair of His mercy. Balancing fear and hope guarantees that they would complement each other. God ﷻ says,

﴿إِنَّمَا يُؤْمِنُ بِآيَاتِنَا الَّذِينَ إِذَا ذُكِّرُوا بِهَا خَرُّوا سُجَّدًا وَسَبَّحُوا بِحَمْدِ رَبِّهِم وَهُمْ لَا يَسْتَكْبِرُونَ ۩﴾

('innamā yu'minu bi-'āyātinā lladhīna 'idhā dhukkirū bihā kharrū sujjadan wa-sabbahū bi-hamdi rabbihim wa-hum lā yastakbirūn[a])

﴿تَتَجَافَىٰ جُنُوبُهُمْ عَنِ الْمَضَاجِعِ يَدْعُونَ رَبَّهُمْ خَوْفًا وَطَمَعًا وَمِمَّا رَزَقْنَاهُمْ يُنفِقُونَ﴾

❨*tatajāfā junūbuhum ʿani l-maḍājiʿi yadʿūna
rabbahum khawfan wa-ṭamaʿan wa-mimmā
razaqnāhum yunfiqūnᵃ*❩

❨*Only those believe in Our signs who, when they are
reminded of them, fall down in prostration and
celebrate the praise of their Lord, and they are not
arrogant. Their sides vacate their beds* to supplicate
their Lord in fear and hope, and they spend out of
what We have provided them*❩88

God ﷻ is both Paramount (*qahhār*) and Forgiving
(*ghaffār*):

﴿قُل إِنَّما أَنا مُنذِرٌ ۖ وَما مِن إِلٰهٍ إِلَّا اللَّهُ الواحِدُ القَهّارُ﴾

❨*qul ʾinnamā ʾana mundhirun wa-mā min ʾilāhin
ʾillā llāhu l-wāḥidu l-qahhārᵘ*❩

﴿رَبُّ السَّماواتِ وَالأَرضِ وَما بَينَهُمَا العَزيزُ الغَفّارُ﴾

---

88 Sūrat al-Sajdah, Verses 15-16.

⌂ After this verse, one must perform a *Sajdah* (prostration).

* That is, they abandon their beds at night and forgo the
pleasure of sleep to worship their Lord in a state of fear and
hope.

⟨*rabbu s-samāwāti wa-l-ʾarḍi wa-mā baynahumā l-ʿazīzu l-ghaffāru*⟩

⟨*Say, 'I am just a warner, and there is no god except God, the One, the Paramount, the Lord of the heavens and the earth and whatever is between them, the Mighty, the Forgiver'*⟩[89]

He ﷻ is Paramount, so no one would become too confident of His grace and mercy. This is because such a person thinks he is safe from God's ﷻ sovereignty and wrath and drowns in sins. As for Forgiving, it means that God forgives often. The doors of His mercy are open to all sinners. For this reason, a person should neither feel despair nor false security:

﴿وَلَا تَيْأَسُوا مِن رَّوْحِ اللَّهِ ۖ إِنَّهُ لَا يَيْأَسُ مِن رَّوْحِ اللَّهِ إِلَّا الْقَوْمُ الْكَافِرُونَ﴾

⟨*wa-lā tayʾasū min rawḥi llāhi ʾinnahū lā yayʾasu min rawḥi llāhi ʾillā l-qawmu l-kāfirūna*⟩

---

[89] Sūrat Ṣād, Verses 65-66.

❝And do not despair of God's mercy. Indeed no one despairs of God's mercy except the faithless lot.❞[90]

﴿أَفَأَمِنُوا مَكْرَ اللَّهِ ۚ فَلَا يَأْمَنُ مَكْرَ اللَّهِ إِلَّا الْقَوْمُ الْخَاسِرُونَ﴾

❝a-fa-'aminū makra llāhi fa-lā ya'manu makra llāhi 'illā l-qawmu l-khāsirūnᵃ❞

❝Do they feel secure from God's devising? No one feels secure from God's devising except the people who are losers❞[91]

Worldly Despair

This means despairing of blessed relief (*al-Faraj al-ilāhī*).

The Cure for Worldly Despair

Optimism

Optimism leads to hope, while pessimism leads to despair and helplessness. From the Prophet ﷺ: "Believing in bad omens is a kind of polytheism (*al-*

---

[90] Sūrat Yūsuf, Verse 87.

[91] Sūrat al-Aʻrāf, Verse 99.

ṭīra shirk)," and "Hope for good, and you will find it."

Supplication

From the Prophet: "Supplication (*al-duʿāʾ*) is the believer's weapon."[92] From Imām ʿAlī ☩: "Supplication is the key."[93] This means that supplication may be an opening that leads to success and an effective method of countering despair.

Hoping For Victory and Divine Aid

If we look at the Noble Qurʾān, we will find that it creates hope in victory for Muslims in many verses. They include the following.

﴿وَلَقَد أَرسَلنا مِن قَبلِكَ في شِيَعِ الأَوَّلينَ﴾

﴾*wa-la-qad ʾarsalnā min qablika fī shiyaʿi l-ʾawwalīnᵃ*﴿

---

92 Kulaynī, Shaykh Muḥammad b. Yaʿqūb, *al-Kāfī*, Vol. 2, p. 468.

93 Ibid.

﴿وَما يَأْتِيهِم مِن رَسُولٍ إِلَّا كانوا بِهِ يَسْتَهْزِئُونَ﴾

﴾*wa-mā ya'tīhim min rasūlin 'illā kānū bihī
yastahzi'ūn*ᵃ﴿

﴿كَذٰلِكَ نَسْلُكُهُ في قُلوبِ المُجْرِمينَ﴾

﴾*ka-dhālika naslukuhū fī qulūbi l-mujrimīn*ᵃ﴿

﴿لا يُؤْمِنونَ بِهِ ۚ وَقَد خَلَت سُنَّةُ الأَوَّلينَ﴾

﴾*lā yu'minūna bihī wa-qad khalat sunnatu l-
'awwalīn*ᵃ﴿

﴾*Certainly We sent [apostles] before you to former
communities, and there did not come to them any
apostle but that they used to deride him. That is how
We let it pass through the hearts of the guilty: they do
not believe in it, and the precedent of the ancients has
already passed*﴿94

The people of misguidance have their methods to
trick people and get them away from the Friends of
God ﷻ. This is not limited to a time or place; it has
existed from the ancient past and will continue to

---

94 Sūrat al-Ḥijr, Verses 10-13.

exist as long as the struggle between truth and falsehood persists. For this reason, we should not be discouraged and should not back down in the face of problems and obstacles. We should not allow despair to make its way into our hearts, and we should not let our enemies' tricks make us lose trust in God ﷻ.

﴿وَلَا تَهِنُوا وَلَا تَحْزَنُوا وَأَنتُمُ الْأَعْلَوْنَ إِن كُنتُم مُؤْمِنِينَ﴾

﴾*wa-lā tahinū wa-lā taḥzanū wa-'antumu l-'aʿlawna 'in kuntum mu'minin*ᵃ﴿

﴿إِن يَمْسَسْكُمْ قَرْحٌ فَقَدْ مَسَّ الْقَوْمَ قَرْحٌ مِثْلُهُ وَتِلْكَ الْأَيَّامُ نُدَاوِلُهَا بَيْنَ النَّاسِ وَلِيَعْلَمَ اللَّهُ الَّذِينَ آمَنُوا وَيَتَّخِذَ مِنكُمْ شُهَدَاءَ وَاللَّهُ لَا يُحِبُّ الظَّالِمِينَ﴾

﴾*'in yamsaskum qarḥun fa-qad massa l-qawma qarḥun mithluhū wa-tilka l-'ayyāmu nudāwiluhā bayna n-nāsi wa-li-yaʿlama llāhu lladhīna 'āmanū wa-yattakhidha minkum shuhadā'a wa-llāhu lā yuḥibbu ẓ-ẓālimin*ᵃ﴿

﴾*Do not weaken or grieve: you shall have the upper hand, should you be faithful. If a wound afflicts you, a like wound has already afflicted those people; and We make such vicissitudes rotate among mankind,* *so that God may ascertain those who have faith, and that He may take martyrs* from among you, and God does not like the wrongdoers*[95]

This verse cautions the Muslims about becoming overwhelmed with grief, despair, and lethargy due to a setback or defeat during battle. Conscious men are those who make lessons out of defeats as well as victories. They identify their weaknesses and strive to achieve decisive victory by fixing gaps in their strategy.

Waiting for the Imām ﷻ and Its Role in Social Reform

When corruption overtakes society, the believer may suffer psychologically. He may imagine that reform is impossible and that striving to uphold his purity is pointless. This may drive a person toward corruption. Hoping for the ultimate reform renews hope in the hearts of the believers and urges them to resist and be patient such that they do not get carried away by their corrupt environment.

---

95 Sūrat Āl 'Imrān, verses 139-140.

* Or 'witnesses.'

Piety and Trust in God

﴿ذَٰلِكُم يوعَظُ بِهِ مَن كانَ يُؤمِنُ بِاللَّهِ وَاليَومِ الآخِرِ ۚ وَمَن يَتَّقِ اللَّهَ يَجعَل لَهُ مَخرَجًا﴾

﴾dhālikum yūʿaẓu bihī man kāna yuʾminu bi-llāhi wa-l-yawmi l-ʾākhiri wa-man yattaqi llāha yajʿal lahū makhraja^n﴿

﴿وَيَرزُقهُ مِن حَيثُ لا يَحتَسِبُ﴾

﴾wa-yarzuqhu min ḥaythu lā yaḥtasibu﴿

﴾To [comply with] this is advised whoever believes in God and the Last Day. And whoever is wary of God, He shall make a way out for him (of the adversities of the world and the Hereafter) and provide for him from whence he does not reckon﴿[96]

From Abī Dharr al-Ghafārī, from the Prophet ﷺ: "I know that there is one verse that would be sufficient for people if they would commit to it: 'Whoever is wary of God, He shall make for him a way out [of the adversities of the world and the

---

[96] Sūrat al-Ṭalāq, Verses 2-3.

Hereafter].' The Prophet repeated this again and again."[97]

In reality, the person who experiences trust in God ﷻ does not allow despair to creep into his determination. He never feels weak when facing problems, no matter how great they are. He continues to resist with firm strength and faith.

From the Prophet ﷺ: "I asked Jibrā'īl, 'What is trusting in God?' He said, 'It knows that the creature cannot harm, benefit, give, or deprive; it is despairing of creatures. If a servant were like this, all his actions would be for God. He would only hope in God and fear no one but God. His only hope would be God. This is trust in God.'"[98]

---

[97] Ṭabrisī, Shaykh Faḍl b. Ḥasan, *Majmaʿ al-Bayān fī Tafsīr al-Qur'ān*, ed. And comm. A committee of expert scholars and editors, Beirut: Mu'assasat al-Aʿlamī lil-Maṭbūʿāt, 1415/1995, 1st ed., Vol. 10, p. 43.

[98] Majlisī, ʿAllamah Muḥammad Bāqir, *Biḥār al-Anwār*, Vol. 66, p. 373.

Knowing that with Hardship There Is Ease

God ﷻ says,

$$﴿فَإِنَّ مَعَ الْعُسْرِ يُسْرًا﴾$$

❨*fa-ʾinna maʿa l-ʿusri yusra[n]*❩

❨*Indeed ease accompanies hardship*❩[99]

From the Prophet ﷺ: "Know that victory accompanies patience, relief accompanies calamity, and ease accompanies hardship. Indeed ease accompanies hardship."[100]

---

[99] Sūrat al-Sharḥ, Verse 5.

[100] Ṣadūq, Shaykh Muḥammad b. ʿAlī, *Man Lā Yaḥḍuruh al-Faqīh*, Vol. 4, p. 413.

The State of the Believer in This World

The goal of the chapter is to highlight the state of the believers and those cheated by the world and urging people not to cling to this world through understanding the following:

1. The believers

2. Those who are cheated by this world

The Commander of the Believers ؏: "Those who truly know the world are like travelers who left an arid home to a fertile one. To reach it, they put up with the difficulty of the road, separation from their friends, the hardships of travel, and the coarseness of the food. They did all this to reach their spacious home and final destination, so they felt no pain, found no expense too much, and loved nothing as they loved things that brought them closer to their home and resting destination. Those who were cheated by this world are like people who used to live in a fertile home but left it for an arid one. Nothing is more hateful and horrible to them than being separated from the things of the past for the things of the future." [101]

---

[101] Sharīf Raḍī, Muḥammad b. al-Ḥusayn, *Nahj al-Balāgha*, p. 397.

Here, Imām ʿAlī ﷺ describes how the believers and unbelievers live in this world and the state of each group.

The Believers

They are "like travelers who left an arid home to a fertile one." The believer concerned about the Hereafter is like a traveler intent on leaving an arid, lifeless land without vegetation or fruits. This land is a metaphor for the world, and believers want to leave it to a fertile land, a metaphor for the Hereafter. On this trip, the believers suffer hardships but can endure them because they want to reach that destination with abundant blessings. Many narrations likened the believer to a traveler. From the Commander of the Believers ﷺ: "God created the world for the sake of what is after it. He tested its people to see which of them were best in conduct. We were not created for this world or commanded to strive in it."[102] He ﷺ also said, "Here are God's prophets and chosen ones: they raised themselves above this world. After them, the righteous followed in their footsteps and viewed the world as carrion prohibited from being eaten except when needed. They ate of this world just

---

[102] Ibid., p. 446.

enough to stay alive and keep their souls in their bodies, and they considered it an extremely foul corpse."[103] For this reason, Imām 'Alī ﷺ described the believers as follows.

"They Put Up With The Difficulty Of The Road."

This world is full of dangers and hardships, and they are not limited to material or physical tribulations. One of the greatest dangers of all is being fooled by this world. This world decorates itself for people, calls them toward it, and makes itself desirable. Those who resist it the most will defeat it. The best metaphor describing this world likens it to a prison. From the Prophet ﷺ: "The world is never a carefree place for a believer; it is his prison and tribulation."[104] From Imām al-Bāqir ﷺ: "Paradise is encircled with hateful things and patience. Whoever is patient over hateful things in this world will go to Paradise. Hell is encircled with

---

[103] Majlisī, 'Allamah Muḥammad Bāqir, *Biḥār al-Anwār*, Vol. 70, p. 111.

[104] al-Hindī, 'Alī al-Muttaqī, *Kanz al-'Ummāl fī Sunan al-Aqwāl wal-Af'āl*, Vol. 3, p. 187.

pleasures and desires. Whoever gives his soul its pleasures and desires will go to Hell."[105]

"Separation from Their Friends"

In this world, the believer is a stranger with no friend to walk this path with because it is a path of hardship and suffering. The absence of friends makes it even harder. However, the believer remains patient to reach the Hereafter and his eternal resting place. From the Commander of the Believers ﷺ: "O people, do not feel lonesome on the path of guidance because its people are few. The people have gathered around a banquet that satisfies but little and leads to much hunger."[106]

"The Hardships of Travel"

If the believer knows that the world is only a passageway and that he is a traveler, he will know that he could never remain in it. This will make him withstand its hardships and difficulties. It has been narrated from the Prophet ﷺ: "Be in this

---

[105] Kulaynī, Shaykh Muḥammad b. Yaʿqūb, *al-Kāfī*,
      Vol. 2, p. 89.

[106] Sharīf Raḍī, Muḥammad b. al-Ḥusayn, *Nahj al-Balāgha*,
      p. 319.

world like a stranger or a passerby, and count yourself among the people of the grave."[107]

"The Coarseness of the Food"

Coarse food is unpalatable food that the soul does not desire. Although a believer makes the most of this world and remembers his share of it, its affairs are not his goal and are not his priority. He can be patient and abstain from these matters if they hinder attaining God's pleasure. Overeating indeed distances a person from God ﷻ. From Imām al-Ṣādiq ؏: "Nothing harms the believer's heart more than overeating. Overeating leads to two things: hard-heartedness and excessive lust."[108]

Whenever food is a delicacy, a person will overeat it. He may even suffer from gluttony (*biṭna*). For this reason, one must be careful and have only as much food as he needs. From the Prophet ﷺ: "Beware of

---

[107] Ṭūsī, Shaykh Muḥammad b. Ḥasan, *al-Amālī*, ed. Mu'assasat al-Biʿtha, Qism al-Dirāsāt al-Islāmiyya, Qom: Dār al-Thaqāfa lil-Ṭibāʿa wal-Nashr wal-Tawzīʿ, 1414, 1ˢᵗ ed., 381.

[108] Majlisī, ʿAllamah Muḥammad Bāqir, *Biḥār al-Anwār*, Vol. 63, p. 337.

gluttony! It corrupts the body, leads to illness, and makes one too lazy to worship."[109]

"To reach their spacious home and their final destination, and so they felt no pain, found no expense too much and loved nothing as they loved things that brought them closer to their home and resting destination." After the Imām ﷺ explained the believer's condition in this world, he ﷺ wanted to explain the believer's contentment with his situation. The believer does not withstand all these hardships and troubles because anyone forces him to do so. He does this while being thankful to God ﷻ and content with his actions. This is because the believer does not feel pain or loss due to a deed that gets him closer to his goal: God's ﷻ pleasure and Paradise. These hardships and troubles are even more desirable to the believer than luxury and bliss if they cause him to attain his goal. This is why the Commander of the Believers also describes them: "They were patient for a few short days that led them to a long rest. It was a profitable trade that their Lord made easy for them. The world wanted them, but they did not want it, and it tried to keep

---

[109] Ibid., Vol. 59, p. 266.

them captive, but they paid the ransom and got away."[110]

Those who are cheated by this world

"Those who were cheated by this world are like people who used to live in a fertile home but left it for an arid one." This image is opposite to that of the believers. The world is the paradise of the unbeliever. The unbeliever also views himself as a traveler but travels from Heaven to Hell. This explains why such a person hates death. The one who only sees this world will see his end as part of its end. When it ends, everything he has will be gone. From Imām al-Ḥasan ﷺ: "The believers feel the greatest pleasure once they are moved from the abode of vexation to eternal bliss. The unbelievers feel the greatest woe once they are moved from paradise to a Fire that does not go out or get extinguished."[111]

---

[110] Sharīf Raḍī, Muḥammad b. al-Ḥusayn, *Nahj al-Balāgha*, p. 304.

[111] Ṣadūq, Shaykh Muḥammad b. ʿAlī, *Maʿānī al-ʾAkhbār*, ed. and comm. ʿAlī Akbar al-Ghaffārī, Qom: Muʾassasat al-Nashr al-Tābiʿa li-Jamāʿat al-Mudarrisīn, 1379AH /1338 SH, p. 288.

"Nothing is more hateful and horrible to them than being separated from the things of the past for the things of the future."

The unbelievers love this world so much that they struggle to escape it. It is one of the hardest things ever for them. Imām Zayn al-ʿĀbidīn ☙ described death and departing from this world as follows: "For the believer, it is like taking off dirty, flea-ridden clothes, and untying heavy restraints and shackles. He replaces them with the most luxurious and best-smelling clothes, pliable mounts, and pleasant homes. For the unbeliever, it is like taking off luxurious clothes and leaving pleasant homes and replacing them with the dirtiest, coarsest clothes, the loneliest houses, and the greatest punishment."[112]

---

[112] Ibid., p. 289.

Tenderness and Righteousness of the Heart

The goal of the chapter is to identify the things that aid in reviving the heart and making it righteous through understanding the following:

1. Tenderheartedness is the door to every kind of righteousness

2. The meaning and scope of tenderheartedness

3. The causes of the hardening and darkening of the heart

4. Curing hard-heartedness

Imām al-Bāqir ﷺ: "Bring about tenderheartedness by engaging in remembrance (*dhikr*) often when you are alone."[113]

Tenderheartedness: the door to every kind of righteousness

A tender heart is a heart that is humble before God's ﷻ greatness. A tender heart is not only a companion to the person but a most excellent

---

[113] Majlisī, ʿAllamah Muḥammad Bāqir, *Biḥār al-Anwār*, Vol. 75, p. 164.

companion. Whoever closely reads the Book of God ﷻ and the blessed biography (*sīra*) of the Prophet ﷺ will find that God ﷻ told his chosen Prophet ﷺ that the worshipers whom God ﷻ loves the most require tenderheartedness. These worshipers are his prophets and their trustees (*awṣiyāʾ*), guides (*hudāt*), people who call others to God ﷻ, students of religious knowledge, and the elites and ordinary people. God ﷻ said,

﴿فَبِمَا رَحْمَةٍ مِنَ اللَّهِ لِنتَ لَهُمْ ۖ وَلَوْ كُنتَ فَظًّا غَلِيظَ القَلْبِ لَانفَضُّوا مِن حَوْلِكَ﴾

﴿*fa-bi-mā raḥmatin mina llāhi linta lahum wa-law kunta fazzan ghalīza l-qalbi la-nfaḍḍū min ḥawlika*﴾

﴿*It is by God's mercy that* you *are gentle to them; and had* you *been harsh and hardhearted, surely they would have scattered from around you*﴾[114]

God ﷻ is saying to the Prophet ﷺ, "If your heart were hard, all these masses would have scattered from around you." From the Commander of the

---

[114] Sūrat Āl ʿImrān, Verse 159.

Believers, "Blessed are those whose hearts are broken for God's sake."[115]

The Meaning and Scope of Tenderheartedness

Tenderheartedness means that a person becomes moved quickly in emotional situations. The outward effects of tenderheartedness include shedding tears. The value of anything in ethics as God ﷻ or Islam views them depends on whether this brings a person closer to God ﷻ. For this reason, tenderheartedness is considered worthless in Islamic ethics unless it is related to God and drawing near Him. It is good if a believer is not careless when God's ﷻ greatness, forgiveness, or punishment is mentioned. The Noble Qur'ān describes itself as follows:

﴿كِتَابًا مُتَشَابِهًا مَثَانِيَ تَقْشَعِرُّ مِنهُ جُلودُ الَّذِينَ يَخْشَونَ رَبَّهُم﴾

﴿*kitāban mutashābihan mathāniya taqsha'irru minhu julūdu lladhīna yakhshawna rabbahum*﴾

---

115 al-Laythī al-Wāsiṭī, Shaykh Kāfī al-Dīn ʿAlī b. Muḥammad, *ʿUyūn al-Ḥikam wal-Mawāʿiẓ*, p. 313.

❨*A scripture [composed] of similar* motifs, whereat quiver the skins of those who fear their Lord*❩[116]

One of the characteristics of God's ﷻ words is that when the believers hear them, their skin trembles, and their bodies shake. This emotional state is a reactive state that affects the body. God ﷻ says about the characteristics of the believers:

❨إِنَّمَا المُؤْمِنُونَ الَّذِينَ إِذَا ذُكِرَ اللَّهُ وَجِلَت قُلُوبُهُم❩

❨*'innamā l-mu'minūna lladhīna 'idhā dhukira llāhu wajilat qulūbuhum*❩

❨*The faithful are only those whose hearts tremble [with awe] when God is mentioned*❩[117]

The qualities of the believer include that his heart trembles when God is mentioned; this is a sign of faith. The believer's heart must feel lowly in the face of the Creator's ﷻ greatness. The believer

---

116 Sūrat al-Zumar, Verse 23.

* Or 'parallel motifs.'

117 Sūrat al-Anfāl, Verse 2.

should even feel ashamed and weep whenever he remembers God's blessings.[118]

The Causes of the Hardening and Darkening of the Heart

Many things cause the heart to become hard. Among them, we mention the following.

Loving This World

God ﷻ says,

﴿وَاصْبِرْ نَفْسَكَ مَعَ الَّذِينَ يَدْعُونَ رَبَّهُم بِالْغَدَاةِ وَالْعَشِيِّ يُرِيدُونَ وَجْهَهُ وَلَا تَعْدُ عَيْنَاكَ عَنْهُم تُرِيدُ زِينَةَ الْحَيَاةِ الدُّنْيَا وَلَا تُطِعْ مَنْ أَغْفَلْنَا قَلْبَهُ عَن ذِكْرِنَا وَاتَّبَعَ هَوَاهُ وَكَانَ أَمْرُهُ فُرُطًا﴾

‹wa-ṣbir nafsaka maʿa lladhīna yadʿūna rabbahum bi-l-ghadāti wa-l-ʿashiyyi yurīdūna wajhahū wa-lā taʿdu ʿaynāka ʿanhum turīdu zīnata l-ḥayāti d-dunyā wa-lā tuṭiʿ man ʾaghfalnā qalbahū ʿan dhikrinā wa-ttabaʿa hawāhu wa-kāna ʾamruhū furuṭaⁿ›

---

118 From a lecture by Āyatullāh Muḥammad Taqī Miṣbāḥ Yazdī, given at the office of Āyatullāh Sayyid ʿAlī Ḥusaynī Khāmineʾī in Qom on August 16, 2011.

❨Content yourself *with the company of those who supplicate their Lord morning and evening, desiring His Face, and* do not lose sight *of them, desiring the glitter of the life of this world.*[*] *And* Do not obey him *whose heart We have made oblivious to Our remembrance, and who follows his own desires, and whose conduct is [mere] profligacy*❩[119]

Loving this world and becoming attached to it corrupts the heart and makes it easy prey for the hosts of Satan. This is why the believer should cut off his attachment to this world. Such an attachment makes the world a goal and an objective in and of itself in place of the Hereafter. The Commander of the Believers ﷺ pointed this out when he said, "Cause it [your heart] to die by being ascetical."[120] Being ascetical means realizing that this world is not the goal but the purpose itself. It ends, and it is only a path to the Hereafter.

---

[119] Sūrat al-Kahf, Verse 28.

[*] Cf. 6:52.

[120] Sharīf Raḍī, Muḥammad b. al-Ḥusayn, *Nahj al-Balāgha*, p. 392.

Sinning

A person's behavior affects the heart. Bad behavior that contradicts the rulings of God ﷻ puts veils on the heart and fills it with darkness. Many Qur'ānic verses emphasize this. They include:

﴿كَلَّا ۖ بَلْ رَانَ عَلَىٰ قُلُوبِهِم مَّا كَانُوا يَكْسِبُونَ﴾

﴿*kallā bal rāna ʿalā qulūbihim mā kānū yaksibūnᵃ*﴾

﴿*No indeed! Rather their hearts have been sullied* by what they have been earning*﴾121

﴿أَوَلَمْ يَهْدِ لِلَّذِينَ يَرِثُونَ الْأَرْضَ مِن بَعْدِ أَهْلِهَا أَن لَّوْ نَشَاءُ أَصَبْنَاهُم بِذُنُوبِهِمْ ۚ وَنَطْبَعُ عَلَىٰ قُلُوبِهِمْ فَهُمْ لَا يَسْمَعُونَ﴾

﴿*'a-wa-lam yahdi li-lladhīna yarithūna l-'arḍa min baʿdi 'ahlihā 'an law nashā'u 'aṣabnāhum bi-dhunūbihim wa-naṭbaʿu ʿalā qulūbihim fa-hum lā yasmaʿūnᵃ*﴾

---

121 Sūrat al-Muṭaffifīn, Verse 14.

* Or 'overcast.'

⟨Does it not dawn upon those who inherited the earth after its [former] inhabitants that if We wish We will punish them for their sins, and set a seal on their hearts so they would not hear?⟩[122]

Abandoning Jihād

﴿وَإِذا أُنزِلَت سورَةٌ أَن آمِنوا بِاللَّهِ وَجاهِدوا مَعَ رَسولِهِ اسْتَأْذَنَكَ أُولُو الطَّوْلِ مِنْهُم وَقالوا ذَرنا نَكُن مَعَ القاعِدينَ﴾

⟨wa-'idhā 'unzilat sūratun 'an 'āminū bi-llāhi wa-jāhidū ma'a rasūlihi sta'dhanaka 'ulū ṭ-ṭawli minhum wa-qālū dharnā nakun ma'a l-qā'idinᵃ⟩

⟨When a sūrah *is sent down [declaring]: 'Have faith in God, and wage* jihād *along with His Apostle, the affluent among them ask* you *for leave, and say, 'Let us remain with those who sit back.'⟩*[123]

Being a bystander when jihād is waged, not defending one's religion, and not standing up to tyrants have dangerous consequences in this world and the Hereafter. The noble verse clearly states that those who sit back when jihād is waged have

---

122 Sūrat al-Aʿrāf, Verse 100.

123 Sūrat al-Tawbah, Verse 86.

had their hearts sealed. Naturally, participating in jihād revives the heart. This is why a person who engages in jihād has more light within him and a softer heart, and he is closer to God ﷻ.

Curing Hard-Heartedness

From the Prophet ﷺ: "The heart is a king and his soldiers. If the king is righteous, his soldiers are righteous; if the king is corrupt, his soldiers are corrupt."[124] Below, we will mention some things that help to enlighten and revive the heart.

The Remembrance of God

﴿إِنَّمَا الْمُؤْمِنُونَ الَّذِينَ إِذَا ذُكِرَ اللَّهُ وَجِلَتْ قُلُوبُهُمْ﴾

❲'innamā l-mu'minūna lladhīna 'idhā dhukira llāhu wajilat qulūbuhum❳

❲The faithful are only those whose hearts tremble [with awe] when God is mentioned❳[125]

---

124 al-Hindī, ʿAlī al-Muttaqī, *Kanz al-ʿUmmāl fī Sunan al-Aqwāl wal-Afʿāl*, Vol. 1, p. 241.

125 Sūrat al-Anfāl, Verse 2.

Imām al-Bāqir ﷺ says, "Bring about tenderheartedness by engaging in remembrance often when you are alone." The meaning of remembrance here is the opposite of heedlessness. It is primarily the engagement of the heart or verbal remembrance that is accompanied by the engagement of the heart. The heart needs remembrance. From the Prophet: "On the day when there is no shade except the shade of God, He will shade seven people [... including] a man who mentioned God in solitude, and his tears flowed out of fear of God."[126]

Wisdom

$$ ﴿يُؤْتِي الْحِكْمَةَ مَن يَشَاءُ ۚ وَمَن يُؤْتَ الْحِكْمَةَ فَقَدْ أُوتِيَ خَيْرًا كَثِيرًا ۗ وَما يَذَّكَّرُ إِلَّا أُولُو الْأَلْبابِ﴾ $$

⟨yu'tī l-ḥikmata man yashā'u wa-man yu'ta l-ḥikmata fa-qad 'ūtiya khayran kathīran wa-mā yadhdhakkaru 'illā 'ulū l-'albāb⟩

---

[126] Ṣadūq, Shaykh Muḥammad b. ʿAlī, *al-Khiṣāl*, corr. and comm. ʿAlī Akbar al-Ghaffārī, Qom: Muʾassasat al-Nashr al-Islāmī al-Tābiʿa li-Jamāʿat al-Mudarrisīn, 1403 AH/1362, p. 392.

❲He gives wisdom to whomever He wishes, and he who is given wisdom, is certainly given an abundant good. But none takes admonition except those who possess intellect❳[127]

From the Commander of the Believers ﷺ: "And enlighten it [your heart] with wisdom."[128] Wisdom is explained by Imām al-Ṣādiq ﷺ as follows: "Wisdom is religious knowledge and learning. Whoever is knowledgeable in religion among you is wise."[129]

Exhortation

From the Commander of the Believers ﷺ: "Revive your heart through exhortation, make it humble by remembering death, and make it admit to annihilation."[130] The exhortation is reminding oneself of the Hereafter. When a person listens to

---

[127] Sūrat al-Baqarah, Verse 269.

[128] Sharīf Raḍī, Muḥammad b. al-Ḥusayn, *Nahj al-Balāgha,* p. 392.

[129] Majlisī, ʿAllamah Muḥammad Bāqir, *Biḥār al-Anwār,* Vol. 1, p. 215.

[130] Sharīf Raḍī, Muḥammad b. al-Ḥusayn, *Nahj al-Balāgha,* p. 392.

an exhortation, he resorts to repentance, which is the life of the heart. This is why we read in Imām al-Sajjād's (Imām Zayn al-ʿĀbidīn) ﷺ supplication: "My God, offenses have clothed me in the garment of my lowliness, separation from Thee has wrapped me in the clothing of my misery! My dreadful crimes have deadened my heart, so bring it to life with repentance from Thee! O, my hope and my aim! O, my wish and my want!"[131]

---

[131] [Translator's note]: Imām Zayn al-ʿĀbidīn ﷺ, *al-Ṣaḥīfa al-Sajjādiyya*, trans. William Chittick, p. 395.

Satan's Steps

The goal of the chapter is to warn against Iblīs' tricks and traps and identifying some ways of confronting him through understanding the following:

1. Who is Satan?

2. Satan's steps and methods.

3. How can we fight Satan?

﴿يا أَيُّهَا الَّذينَ آمَنوا لا تَتَّبِعوا خُطُواتِ الشَّيطانِ ۚ وَمَن يَتَّبِعخُطُواتِ الشَّيطانِ فَإِنَّهُ يَأْمُرُ بِالفَحشاءِ وَالمُنكَرِ﴾

⟨yā-'ayyuhā lladhīna 'āmanū lā tattabi'ū khuṭuwāti sh-shayṭāni wa-man yattabi' khuṭuwāti sh-shayṭāni fa-'innahū ya'muru bi-l-faḥshā'i wa-l-munkari⟩

⟨O you who have faith! Do not follow in Satan's steps. Whoever follows in Satan's steps [should know that] he indeed prompts [you to commit] indecent acts and wrong⟩[132]

---

[132] Sūrat al-Nūr, Verse 21.

Who Is Satan?

The word Shayṭān (Satan) in Arabic is linguistically related to the words "sh.ṭ.n" and "*shāṭin*." It means the contemptible malicious one. "Shayṭān" is used to refer to a rebellious, disobedient creature, whether it is a human or a nonhuman. The word also means an evil spirit that is away from the Truth. Shayṭān is a common noun, and Iblīs is a proper noun for Satan.[133]

In many of its verses, the Holy Qur'ān tells us that Satan is man's first enemy:

﴿إِنَّ الشَّيطانَ لَكُم عَدُوٌّ فَاتَّخِذوهُ عَدُوًّا ۚ إِنَّما يَدعو حِزبَهُ لِيَكونوا مِن أَصحابِ السَّعيرِ﴾

﴾inna sh-shayṭāna lakum ʿaduwwun fa-ttakhidhūhu ʿaduwwan ʾinnamā yadʿū ḥizbahū li-yakūnū min ʾaṣḥābi s-saʿīr﴿

---

133 Shīrāzī, Āyatullāh Nāṣir Makārim, *Mukhtaṣar al-Amthal fī Tafsīr Kitāb Allāh al-Munzal*, Qom: Madrasat al-Imām ʿAlī b. Abī Ṭalib, 1426 AH, 1st ed., Vol. 1, p. 171.

❲Satan is indeed your enemy, so treat him as an enemy. He only invites his confederates so that they may be among the inmates of the Blaze❳[134]

He is cursed by God ﷻ for his arrogance and refusal to prostrate himself to Ādam ؉. He is also the first to display zeal (*ḥamiyya*) and bigotry (*'aṣabiyya*). God ﷻ says,

﴿وَإِذ قُلنا لِلمَلائِكَةِ اسجُدوا لِآدَمَ فَسَجَدوا إِلّا إِبليسَ أَبى وَاستَكبَرَ وَكانَ مِنَ الكافِرينَ﴾

❲wa-'idh qulnā li-l-malā'ikati sjudū li-'ādama fa-sajadū 'illā 'iblīsa 'abā wa-stakbara wa-kāna mina l-kāfirīnᵃ❳

❲And when We said to the angels, 'Prostrate before Adam,' they prostrated, but not Iblis: he refused and acted arrogantly, and he was one of the faithless❳[135]

Imām 'Alī ؉ says, "The angels prostrated, all of them together, except Iblīs. He was seized with zeal, so he boasted about his creation to Ādam, and he acted with bigotry toward Ādam due to his origin.

---

134 Sūrat Fāṭir, Verse 6.

135 Sūrat al-Baqarah, Verse 34.

The Enemy of God (Satan) is the Imām of the bigots and the ancestor of the arrogant. He planted the seeds of bigotry and tried to compete with God over His might."[136] The Qurʾānic usage of the word Satan also includes human beings who have a corrupting influence and are enemies of the divine message.

Satan's Steps and Methods

The first and most important mission that Satan took upon himself was to drive Man away from the straight path and drag him down to the lowest of the low (*asfal sāfilīn*). God ﷻ describes him as saying,

﴿قَالَ فَبِمَا أَغْوَيْتَنِي لَأَقْعُدَنَّ لَهُمْ صِرَاطَكَ الْمُسْتَقِيمَ﴾

﴾qāla fa-bi-mā ʾaghwaytanī la-ʾaqʿudanna lahum
ṣirāṭaka l-mustaqīmᵃ﴿

﴿ثُمَّ لَآتِيَنَّهُم مِّن بَيْنِ أَيْدِيهِمْ وَمِنْ خَلْفِهِمْ وَعَنْ أَيْمَانِهِمْ وَعَن شَمَائِلِهِمْ ۖ وَلَا تَجِدُ أَكْثَرَهُمْ شَاكِرِينَ﴾

---

136 Sharīf Raḍī, Muḥammad b. al-Ḥusayn, *Nahj al-Balāgha*, p. 286.

❲*thumma la-'ātiyannahum min bayni 'aydīhim
wa-min khalfihim wa-'an 'aymānihim wa-'an
shamā'ilihim wa-lā tajidu 'aktharahum shākirīn*[a]❳

❲*'As You have consigned me to perversity,' he said, 'I
will surely lie in wait for them on Your straight path.
Then I will come at them from their front and from
their rear, and from their right and their left, and
You will not find most of them to be grateful.'*❳[137]

However, God strictly forbade us from following
his steps:

﴿يا أَيُّهَا الَّذينَ آمَنوا لا تَتَّبِعوا خُطُواتِ الشَّيطانِ وَمَن
يَتَّبِعخُطُواتِ الشَّيطانِ فَإِنَّهُ يَأمُرُ بِالفَحشاءِ وَالمُنكَرِ﴾

❲*yā-'ayyuhā lladhīna 'āmanū lā tattabi'ū
khuṭuwāti sh-shayṭāni wa-man yattabi' khuṭuwāti
sh-shayṭāni fa-'innahū ya'muru bi-l-faḥshā'i wa-l-
munkari*❳

❲*O you who have faith! Do not follow in Satan's
steps. Whoever follows in Satan's steps [should know*

---

[137] Sūrat al-A'rāf, Verses 16-17.

that] he indeed prompts [you to commit] indecent acts and wrong⟩[138]

The Meaning of Following Satan's Steps

'Allāma Ṭabāṭabā'ī says that the meaning of following Satan's footsteps is not following him in matters of falsehood. It specifically means following him in religious matters. He causes this by decorating falsehood to make it look like the truth and by pretending that things that have nothing to do with religion are a part of religion. This causes people to uphold these things without knowing the truth about them:[139]

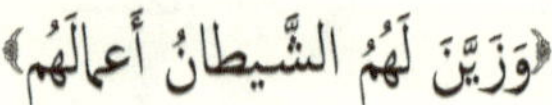

⟨wa-zayyana lahumu sh-shayṭānu 'a'mālahum⟩

⟨And Satan has made their deeds seem decorous to them⟩[140]

---

[138] Sūrat al-Nūr, Verse 21.

[139] Ṭabāṭabā'ī, 'Allamah Sayyid Muḥammad Ḥusayn, *al-Mīzān fī Tafsīr al-Qur'ān*, Qom: Mu'assasat al-Nashr al-Islāmī, 1417 AH, 5th ed., Vol. 2, p. 101.

[140] Sūrat al-Naml, Verse 24.

When a person takes their first steps with Satan, he continues on this path until Satan leads him to perdition. The Commander of the Believers ﷻ says, "They gave Satan possession of their affairs, and he took them as his prey. He laid his eggs and had his spawn in their breasts, and he crawled and took his first steps within them. He looked out through their eyes and spoke through their tongues, leading them to missteps and making rashness seem decorous to them."[141]

The most significant causes that allow Satan entry into the soul include:

Following One's Desires

This was one of Satan's most important characteristics. He wanted to worship God ﷻ the way he pleased. About this, Imām al-Ṣādiq ﷺ says, "God commanded Iblīs to prostrate himself to Ādam, so he said, 'O Lord, if you spare me from prostrating myself to Ādam, I will worship you as You have never been worshiped before.' God said,

---

[141] Sharīf Raḍī, Muḥammad b. al-Ḥusayn, *Nahj al-Balāgha*, p. 53.

'It pleases me to be obeyed in the way that I choose to be obeyed."[142]

Being Prideful and Belittling One's Sins

From the Prophet ﷺ: "Mūsā said to Iblīs, 'Tell me the sin that causes you to take hold of the children of Ādam if they commit it.' Iblīs said, 'That happens when they become prideful, think of their acts of worship as grand, and view their sins as minor."[143]

Women, Alcohol, and Money

From Imām 'Alī ؏: "There are three tribulations: loving women, which is Satan's sword; drinking wine, which is Satan's trap; and loving money, which is Satan's arrow."[144]

---

142 Majlisī, 'Allamah Muḥammad Bāqir, *Biḥār al-Anwār*, Vol. 2, p. 262.

143 Kulaynī, Shaykh Muḥammad b. Ya'qūb, *al-Kāfī*, Vol. 2, p. 314.

144 Ṣadūq, Shaykh Muḥammad b. 'Alī, *al-Khiṣāl*, p. 113.

Anger

From Imām al-Bāqir ﷺ: "Anger is an ember from Satan that burns within the heart of the children of Ādam. This is why whenever one of you becomes angry, your eyes become red, your veins bulge, and Satan finds his way into you."[145]

How Can We Fight Satan?

Satan is man's eternal enemy and is in constant and continuous war with man. For this reason, the first steps of facing Satan include knowing that Satan is man's biggest enemy and that he strives to create animosity between him and others. God ﷻ said,

﴿إِنَّمَا يُرِيدُ الشَّيطَانُ أَن يُوقِعَ بَينَكُمُ العَدَاوَةَ وَالبَغضَاءَ﴾

*⟨'innamā yurīdu sh-shayṭānu 'an yūqi'a
baynakumu l-'adāwata wa-l-baghḍā'a⟩*

*⟨Indeed Satan seeks to cast enmity and
hatred among you⟩[146]*

---

145 Kulaynī, Shaykh Muḥammad b. Ya'qūb, *al-Kāfī*,
    Vol. 2, p. 305.

146 Sūrat al-Mā'idah, Verse 91.

﴿إِنَّ الشَّيْطَانَ لَكُمَا عَدُوٌّ مُبِينٌ﴾

❲*'inna sh-shayṭāna lakumā 'aduwwun mubīnᵘⁿ*❳

❲*"Satan is indeed your manifest enemy"*❳[147]

Many steps and ways can help man face Satan and protect him from Satanic tricks. They include the following:

Engaging in the Remembrance of God

From the Commander of the Believers ﷺ: "I testify that there is no god but God alone who has no partner... This is the support of faith, the door to benevolence (*iḥsān*), the way to please God and the method of driving away Satan."[148]

Prostrating For Long

From the Prophet ﷺ: "Prostrate for long. Nothing is heavier to Iblīs than seeing the Children of Ādam prostrating. It is because he was commanded to prostrate himself, but he disobeyed, whereas the

---

[147] Sūrat al-A'rāf, Verse 22.

[148] Sharīf Raḍī, Muḥammad b. al-Ḥusayn, *Nahj al-Balāgha*, p. 46.

Children of Ādam were commanded to prostrate themselves, and they obeyed."[149] From Imām al-Ṣādiq ﷺ: "Whenever a servant prostrates himself for a long time, Iblīs calls out, 'Woe to me. He obeyed, and I disobeyed, and he prostrated himself while I refused.'"[150]

Worship

From the Prophet ﷺ: "Shall I tell you of deeds that cause Satan to be as far away from you as the East is far from the West?" Those present said, "Yes." He ﷺ said, "Fasting blackens his face, charity (*ṣadaqa*) breaks his back, loving others for God's sake and cooperating to do good works puts an end to him, and seeking forgiveness slices his jugular vein."[151]

---

[149] Ṣadūq, Shaykh Muḥammad b. ʿAlī, *ʿIlal al-Sharāiʿ*, intro. Sayyid Muḥammad Ṣadiq Baḥr al-ʿUlūm, Najaf: al-Maktaba al-Ḥaydariyya, 1385/1966, Vol. 2, p. 34.

[150] Kulaynī, Shaykh Muḥammad b. Yaʿqūb, *al-Kāfī*, Vol. 3, p. 264.

[151] Ṣadūq, Shaykh Muḥammad b. ʿAlī, *al-Amālī*, Qom: Muʾassasat al-Biʿtha, 1417, 1st ed., 117.

Keeping a Qur'ān at Home and Reciting It

From Imām al-Ṣādiq ﷺ: "Nothing is heavier on Satan than silently reciting the Qur'ān. Having a Qur'ān at home drives Satan away."[152]

---

[152] Majlisī, 'Allamah Muḥammad Bāqir, *Biḥār al-Anwār*, Vol. 89, p. 201.

The Consequences of Sins after Death

The goal of the chapter is to mention the consequences of sins and the fate of the disobedient and the unbelievers in the isthmus (*ʿālam al-barzakh*) through understanding the following:

1. The consequences of sins in the isthmus.

2. The consequences of sins in the Hereafter.

3. Bad deeds manifest themselves in horrible images.

﴿يَومَ تَجِدُ كُلُّ نَفسٍ ما عَمِلَت مِن خَيرٍ مُحضَرًا وَما عَمِلَت مِن سوءٍ تَوَدُّ لَو أَنَّ بَينَها وَبَينَهُ أَمَدًا بَعيدًا ۗ وَيُحَذِّرُكُمُ اللَّهُ نَفسَهُ ۗ وَاللَّهُ رَءوفٌ بِالعِبادِ﴾

﴿yawma tajidu kullu nafsin mā ʿamilat min khayrin muḥḍaran wa-mā ʿamilat min sūʾin tawaddu law ʾanna baynahā wa-baynahū ʾamadan baʿīdan wa-yuḥadhdhirukumu llāhu nafsahū wa-llāhu raʾūfun bi-l-ʿibādi﴾

﴿The day when every soul will find present whatever good it has done; and as to whatever evil it has done it will wish there were a far distance between it and

itself. God warns you to beware of [disobeying] Him, and God is most kind to [His] servants[153]

The Consequences of Sins in the Isthmus

From Imām al-Ṣādiq ﷺ: "The isthmus is the grave: it is the abode of reward and punishment between this world and the Hereafter."[154] The following constitute the most critical consequences of sins in the Hereafter.

The Throes of Death

﴿وَجَاءَت سَكْرَةُ المَوتِ بِالحَقِّ ۖ ذَٰلِكَ ما كُنتَ مِنهُ تَحِيدُ﴾

﴿wa-jā'at sakratu l-mawti bi-l-ḥaqqi dhālika mā kunta minhu taḥīd^u﴾

---

[153] Sūrat Āl 'Imrān, Verse 30.

[154] al-Ḥuwayzī, al-'Arūsī, *Tafsīr Nūr al-Thaqalayn*, corr. and comm. Sayyid Hāshim al-Rasūlī al-Muḥillātī, Qom: Mu'assasat Ismā'īlyān, 1412 AH/1370 SH, 4th ed., Vol. 3, p. 553.

⟨Then the agony of death brings the truth: 'This is what you used to shun!'⟩*[155]

From the Commander of the Believers ﷺ: "Any Shīʿī who commits a deed that we had forbidden will be tried to be cleansed of his sin. He will be tested on his money, children, and himself. This way, he meets God sinless. If any of his sins remain, his death will be heavier."[156]

The Loneliness of the Grave

From the Commander of the Believers ﷺ: "O servants of God, what comes after death for those who are not forgiven is worse than death: it is the grave. Beware its narrowness and wretchedness and darkness and loneliness."[157]

Some texts signify that it is commendable to lay the dead into the grave slowly. It was narrated by Imām al-Ṣādiq ﷺ: "When you carry the dead person into

---

[155] Sūrat Qāf, Verse 19.

* Or 'when the agony of death arrives with the truth.'

[156] Majlisī, ʿAllamah Muḥammad Bāqir, *Biḥār al-Anwār*, Vol. 6, p. 157.

[157] Ibid., Vol. 6, p. 218.

his grave, do not lower him into it suddenly. Great terrors await in the grave. Let the one carrying the dead seek God's refuge from the gravity of the Hereafter, put the dead person near the grave's edge, and give him some time. He should move the dead person further and give him time to prepare himself. After that, the dead should be put at the grave's edge."[158]

The Squeeze of the Grave

It may be understood from the narrations that this phenomenon differs from one person to another based on the depth of his faith and his deeds in this world. Another proof is that some narrations have stated that performing certain deeds spares one from the squeeze of the grave.

From Abū Baṣīr, from Imām al-Ṣādiq ﷺ: "I said, 'May I be made ransom to you. What about the squeeze of the grave?' He said, 'It does not affect the believers. Different spots of the earth boast to one another, saying, 'A believer stepped on me, but not on you.' The earth tells the believer, 'By God, I used to love you when you walked up on me [in

---

[158] Ṣadūq, Shaykh Muḥammad b. ʿAlī, *Man Lā Yaḥḍuruh al-Faqīh*, Vol. 1, p. 170

life]. Now that I am entrusted with you, you will see how I will treat you.' Then the earth will open itself up as far as the believer's eyes can see.'"[159] The narrations also state that certain deeds lead to suffering the squeeze of the grave or to it being more severe. They include the narration from the Commander of the Believers ﷺ: "The punishment of the grave comes from gossiping, not purifying oneself of urine, and abandoning[160] one's wife."[161]

The Consequences of Sins in the Hereafter

The most critical consequences of sins and acts of disobedience in the Hereafter include:

Being Deserving of Hellfire

God ﷻ said,

﴿بَلىٰ مَن كَسَبَ سَيِّئَةً وَأَحاطَت بِهِ خَطيئَتُهُ فَأُولٰئِكَ أَصحابُ النّارِ ۖ هُم فيها خالِدونَ﴾

---

[159] Ibid.

[160] This is when a man abandons his bed and food while being unjust to his wife.

[161] Ṣadūq, Shaykh Muḥammad b. ʻAlī, *ʻIlal al-Sharāiʻ*, Vol. 1, p. 309.

❨*balā man kasaba sayyi'atan wa-'aḥāṭat bihī
khaṭī'atuhū fa-'ulā'ika 'aṣḥābu n-nāri hum fīhā
khālidūn*ᵃ❩

❨*Certainly whoever commits misdeeds and is
besieged by his iniquity —such shall be the inmates of
the Fire, and they shall remain in it [forever]*❩[162]

❨وَعَدَ اللَّهُ الْمُنَافِقِينَ وَالْمُنَافِقَاتِ وَالْكُفَّارَ نَارَ جَهَنَّمَ خَالِدِينَ فِيهَا
هِيَ حَسْبُهُمْ ۚ وَلَعَنَهُمُ اللَّهُ ۖ وَلَهُمْ عَذَابٌ مُقِيمٌ❩

❨*wa'ada llāhu l-munāfiqīna wa-l-munāfiqāti wa-l-
kuffāra nāra jahannama khālidīna fīhā hiya
ḥasbuhum wa-la'anahumu llāhu wa-lahum
'adhābun muqīm*ᵘⁿ❩

❨*God has promised the hypocrites, men and women,
and the faithless, the Fire of hell, to remain in it
[forever]. That suffices them. God has cursed them,
and there is a lasting punishment for them*❩[163]

From Imām Mūsā al-Kāẓim ﷺ: "God only decrees
an eternity in the Fire for the unbelievers, the
ungrateful [to God], the people of misguidance,

---

[162] Sūrat al-Baqarah, Verse 81.

[163] Sūrat al-Tawbah, Verse 68.

and polytheists."[164] A sinning unbeliever is not included in any of these categories.

Being Scandalized in the Hereafter

God ﷻ said,

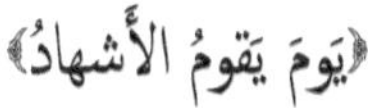

(yawma yaqūmu l-'ashhād^u)

(on the day when the witnesses rise up)[165]

The verse states that this day is when things are laid down in God's presence, and all secrets are revealed for all to see. No scandal can be worse than the scandal on this day, and no victory is better than victory on this day. It is when God ﷻ will champion the prophets and increase their favor and when He will scandalize the unbelievers and leave the unjust to their evil end.

---

164 Majlisī, 'Allamah Muḥammad Bāqir, *Biḥār al-Anwār*, Vol. 8, p. 351.

165 Sūrat Ghāfir, Verse 51.

Being Humiliated

On the Day of Judgment, the disobedient will suffer humiliation, as in verse:

﴿خَاشِعَةً أَبصارُهُم تَرهَقُهُم ذِلَّةٌ وَقَد كانوا يُدعَونَ إِلَى السُّجودِ وَهُم سالِمونَ﴾

⟨khāshiʿatan ʾabṣāruhum tarhaquhum dhillatun wa-qad kānū yudʿawna ʾilā s-sujūdi wa-hum sālimūnᵃ⟩

⟨With a humbled look [in their eyes], they will be overcast by abasement. Certainly they were summoned to prostrate themselves while they were yet sound⟩166

Being Regretful

One of the descriptions of the Day of Resurrection is that it is the day of regret. God ﷻ said,

﴿وَأَنذِرهُم يَومَ الحَسرَةِ إِذ قُضِيَ الأَمرُ وَهُم في غَفلَةٍ وَهُم لا يُؤمِنونَ﴾

---

166 Sūrat al-Qalam, Verse 43.

❨*wa-'andhirhum yawma l-ḥasrati 'idh quḍiya l-
'amru wa-hum fī ghaflatin wa-hum lā yu'minūn*ᵃ❩

❨*Warn them of the Day of Regret*, when the matter
will be decided, while they are [yet] heedless and do
not have faith*❩167

Having Bad Deeds Manifest as Horrible Images

The consequences of sins in the Hereafter include
that they will manifest as images equivalent to the
sin. God ﷻ said,

﴿يَوْمَ تَجِدُ كُلُّ نَفْسٍ مَا عَمِلَتْ مِن خَيْرٍ مُحْضَرًا وَمَا عَمِلَتْ مِن
سُوءٍ تَوَدُّ لَوْ أَنَّ بَيْنَهَا وَبَيْنَهُ أَمَدًا بَعِيدًا وَيُحَذِّرُكُمُ اللَّهُ نَفْسَهُ وَاللَّهُ
رَءُوفٌ بِالْعِبَادِ﴾

❨*yawma tajidu kullu nafsin mā 'amilat min
khayrin muḥḍaran wa-mā 'amilat min sū'in
tawaddu law 'anna baynahā wa-baynahū
'amadan ba'īdan wa-yuḥadhdhirukumu llāhu
nafsahū wa-llāhu ra'ūfun bi-l-'ibādⁱ*❩

---

167 Sūrat Maryam, Verse 39.

* Another name for the Day of Judgement.

⟪The day when every soul will find (tajidu) present whatever good it has done; and as to whatever evil it has done it will wish there were a far distance between it and itself. God warns you to beware of [disobeying] Him, and God is most kind to [His] servants⟫[168]

This verse indicates that good and bad deeds manifest on the Day of Resurrection. A person will see all his good and bad deeds with his own eyes. Those who see their good deeds will be happy and hopeful, and those who see their bad deeds will be frightened. The latter will wish that they could be distant from these sins. The verse did not state that sinners wished their bad deeds would perish. This is because they know that nothing perishes in that world.

For this reason, they wish to put a distance between themselves and these deeds. No matter how few one is good or bad deeds are, they will be manifest on the Day of Resurrection. This is consistent with

---

[168] Sūrat Āl ʿImrān, Verse 30.

the verb *"tajidu;"* *wujūd* is the opposite of nonexistence (*'adam*).[169]

---

[169] See: Shīrāzī, Āyatullāh Nāṣir Makārim, *Mukhtaṣar al-Amthal fī Tafsīr Kitāb Allāh al-Munzal.*, Vol. 2, p. 463 (paraphrased).

Happiness in Islam

The goal of the chapter is to explain the concept of happiness and its importance in Islam, and explaining the things that lead to achieving it through understanding the following:

1. Happiness in this world and the Hereafter.

2. The conditions of worldly happiness.

3. The signs of happiness.

4. Concepts related to happiness.

﴿يَوْمَ يَأْتِ لَا تَكَلَّمُ نَفْسٌ إِلَّا بِإِذْنِهِ ۚ فَمِنْهُم شَقِيٌّ وَسَعِيدٌ﴾

﴿yawma ya'ti lā takallamu nafsun 'illā bi-'idhnihī
fa-minhum shaqiyyun wa-saʿīd^{un}﴾

﴿فَأَمَّا الَّذِينَ شَقُوا فَفِي النَّارِ لَهُمْ فِيها زَفِيرٌ وَشَهِيقٌ﴾

﴿fa-'ammā lladhīna shaqū fa-fī n-nāri lahum fīhā
zafīrun wa-shahīq^{un}﴾

﴿خَالِدِينَ فِيها ما دَامَتِ السَّمَاوَاتُ وَالْأَرْضُ إِلَّا ما شَاءَ رَبُّكَ ۚ
إِنَّ رَبَّكَ فَعَّالٌ لِمَا يُرِيدُ﴾

❲*khālidīna fīhā mā dāmati s-samāwātu wa-l-ʾarḍu ʾillā mā shāʾa rabbuka ʾinna rabbaka faʿʿālun li-mā yurīdᵘ*❳

❲وَأَمَّا الَّذِينَ سُعِدُوا فَفِي الْجَنَّةِ خَالِدِينَ فِيهَا مَا دَامَتِ السَّمَاوَاتُ وَالْأَرْضُ إِلَّا مَا شَاءَ رَبُّكَ ۖ عَطَاءً غَيْرَ مَجْذُوذٍ❳

❲*wa-ʾammā lladhīna suʿidū fa-fī l-jannati khālidīna fīhā mā dāmati s-samāwātu wa-l-ʾarḍu ʾillā mā shāʾa rabbuka ʿaṭāʾan ghayra majdhūdhⁿ*❳

❲*The day it comes, no one shall speak except by His leave. [On that day,] some of them will be wretched and [some] felicitous. As for the wretched, they shall be in the Fire: their lot therein will be groaning and wailing. They shall remain in it for as long as the heavens and the earth endure —except what your Lord may wish; indeed your Lord does whatever He desires. As for the felicitous, they will be in paradise. They will remain in it for as long as the heavens and the earth endure —except what your Lord may wish — an endless bounty*❳[170]

---

[170] Sūrat Hūd, Verses 105-108.

Happiness in This World and the Hereafter

The holy verses refer to two forms of happiness that man aspires to: one is related to this world, and the second is related to the Hereafter. This is where people differ from one another. Some consider their happiness limited to the world's delicacies and pleasures only. This kind of happiness is an illusion that will eventually fade away. Others consider their happiness related to the Hereafter. They believe that anything related to that eternal happiness leads to their true happiness and contentment. This is what true happiness is.

Islam is a comprehensive system. It set rules and regulations for man to order his life in this world and the Hereafter.

Worldly happiness: Islam legislated rules and regulations that ensure man's happiness regarding his relation to himself and others. Examples include Islam's prohibition of drinking wine, listening to songs, gambling, and doing drugs. They also include the obligations of Islam, such as praying, fasting, and upholding blood relations (*ṣilat al-raḥim*). The latter are deeds that have positive consequences. These rulings guarantee a happy life, and the Noble Qurʾān emphasizes that

this worldly life is only a way to attain eternal life.
God ﷻ said,

$$﴿مَن عَمِلَ صَالِحًا مِن ذَكَرٍ أَو أُنثَىٰ وَهُوَ مُؤمِنٌ فَلَنُحيِيَنَّهُ حَيَاةً طَيِّبَةً ۖ وَلَنَجزِيَنَّهُم أَجرَهُم بِأَحسَنِ مَا كَانُوا يَعمَلُونَ﴾$$

*﴿man ʿamila ṣāliḥan min dhakarin ʾaw ʾunthā wa-
huwa muʾminun fa-la-nuḥyiyannahū ḥayātan
ṭayyibatan wa-la-najziyannahum ʾajrahum bi-
ʾaḥsani mā kānū yaʿmalūnᵃ﴾*

*﴿Whoever acts righteously, [whether] male or
female, should he be faithful, —We shall revive him
with a good life and pay them their reward by the
best of what they used to do﴾*[171]

He ﷻ also said,

$$﴿وَابتَغِ فِيمَا آتَاكَ اللَّهُ الدَّارَ الآخِرَةَ ۖ وَلَا تَنسَ نَصِيبَكَ مِنَ الدُّنيَا﴾$$

*﴿wa-btaghi fī-mā ʾātāka llāhu d-dāra l-ʾākhirata
wa-lā tansa naṣībaka mina d-dunyā﴾*

---

[171] Sūrat al-Naḥl, Verse 97.

❨*By the means of what God has given you, seek the abode of the Hereafter, while not forgetting your share of this world*❩172

Happiness in the Hereafter is true: it is eternal and depends on man's good deeds. God ﷻ said,

﴿الَّذِينَ تَتَوَفَّاهُمُ الْمَلَائِكَةُ طَيِّبِينَ ۙ يَقُولُونَ سَلَامٌ عَلَيْكُمُ ادْخُلُوا الْجَنَّةَ بِمَا كُنتُمْ تَعْمَلُونَ﴾

❨*alladhīna tatawaffāhumu l-malā'ikatu ṭayyibīna yaqūlūna salāmun 'alaykumu dkhulū l-jannata bi-mā kuntum ta'malūnª*❩

❨*Those whom the angels take away while they are pure. They say [to them], 'Peace be to you! Enter paradise because of what you used to do.'*❩173

and

﴿لِّلَّذِينَ أَحْسَنُوا فِي هَٰذِهِ الدُّنْيَا حَسَنَةٌ ۚ وَلَدَارُ الْآخِرَةِ خَيْرٌ ۚ وَلَنِعْمَ دَارُ الْمُتَّقِينَ﴾

---

172 Sūrat al-Qaṣaṣ, Verse 77.

173 Sūrat al-Naḥl, Verse 32.

*(li-lladhīna ʾaḥsanū fī hādhihi d-dunyā ḥasanatun
wa-la-dāru l-ʾākhirati khayrun wa-la-niʿma dāru
l-muttaqīnᵃ)*

*(For those who do good in this world there will be a
good [reward], and the abode of the Hereafter is
better, and the abode of the Godwary is surely
excellent)*[174]

The Prophet ﷺ said, "The truly happy person is the one who chose an eternal abode whose blessings are everlasting over a perishing abode whose suffering never ends. The happy person offers his money in this world for the sake of the Hereafter rather than leaving it behind for other people who will be happy to spend it while he toiled to save it."[175]

The Conditions of Worldly Happiness

Certain things contribute to psychological happiness and contentment. They include:

---

174 Sūrat al-Naḥl, Verse 30.

175 Majlisī, ʿAllamah Muḥammad Bāqir, *Biḥār al-Anwār*, Vol. 74, p. 188.

Faith and Good Deeds

God ﷻ said,

$$\llangle الَّذِينَ آمَنوا وَلَم يَلبِسوا إِيمانَهُم بِظُلمٍ أُولئِكَ لَهُمُ الأَمنُ وَهُم مُهتَدونَ \rrangle$$

⟨*alladhīna 'āmanū wa-lam yalbisū 'īmānahum bi-ẓulmin 'ulā'ika lahumu l-'amnu wa-hum muhtadūn*ᵃ⟩

⟨*Those who have faith and do not taint their faith with wrongdoing —for such there shall be safety, and they are the [rightly] guided.*⟩[176]

From the Commander of the Believers ؑ: "Through faith, one reaches the peak of happiness."[177]

---

[176] Sūrat al-Anʿām, Verse 82.

[177] al-Laythī al-Wāsiṭī, Shaykh Kāfī al-Dīn ʿAlī b. Muḥammad, *ʿUyūn al-Ḥikam wal-Mawāʿiẓ*, p. 189.

Engaging in the Remembrance of God

God ﷻ said,

﴿الَّذِينَ آمَنُوا وَتَطْمَئِنُّ قُلُوبُهُم بِذِكْرِ اللَّهِ ۗ
أَلَا بِذِكْرِ اللَّهِ تَطْمَئِنُّ الْقُلُوبُ﴾

﴾*ªlladhīna 'āmanū wa-taṭma'innu qulūbuhum bi-
dhikri llāhi 'a-lā bi-dhikri llāhi taṭma'innu l-
qulūb*ᵘ﴿

﴾*those who have faith, and whose hearts find rest in
the remembrance of God.' Look! The hearts find rest
in God's remembrance!*﴿[178]

Being heedless of remembering God leads to
wretchedness: such a person experiences distress
and misery. God ﷻ says,

﴿وَمَنْ أَعْرَضَ عَن ذِكْرِي فَإِنَّ لَهُ مَعِيشَةً ضَنكًا﴾

﴾*wa-man 'a'raḍa 'an dhikrī fa-'inna lahū
ma'īshatan ḍankan*﴿

---

[178] Ṣūrat al-Ra'd, Verse 28.

*⟨But whoever disregards My remembrance,
his shall be a wretched life⟩*[179]

Sitting With the People of Knowledge

From the Commander of the Believers ﷻ: "Sit with the people of knowledge, and you will find happiness."[180] This is because sitting with people of knowledge is beneficial at the level of the heart and learning.

Holding the Soul Accountable for Its Actions

From the Commander of the Believers ﷻ: "Whoever tires his soul by rectifying it will be happy, and whoever neglects his soul's indulgence in its desires will be wretched and distant from God."[181]

---

[179] Sūrat Ṭā Hā, Verse 128.

[180] al-Laythī al-Wāsiṭī, Shaykh Kāfī al-Dīn ʿAlī b. Muḥammad, *ʿUyūn al-Ḥikam wal-Mawāʿiẓ*, p. 221.

[181] Ibid., p. 445.

The Signs of Happiness

Man's happiness has signs, including:

Not Putting Stock in This World
The Prophet ﷺ: "If a person is deserving of happiness and God's guardianship, death is made the focus, and hope is put behind. If a person is deserving of misery and Satan's guardianship, hope is made the focus, and death is put behind."[182]

Continuous Worship

From the Commander of the Believers ؏: "Continuous worship is proof of [otherworldly] happiness."[183]

Sincerity

From the Commander of the Believers ؏: "Being sincere in one's deeds is a sign of happiness."[184]

---

[182] Kulaynī, Shaykh Muḥammad b. Yaʿqūb, *al-Kāfī*, Vol. 3, p. 258.

[183] al-Laythī al-Wāsiṭī, Shaykh Kāfī al-Dīn ʿAlī b. Muḥammad, *ʿUyūn al-Ḥikam wal-Mawāʿiẓ*, p. 251.

[184] Ibid., p. 70.

God ﷻ said about those who wasted their works away,

﴿قُل هَل نُنَبِّئُكُم بِالأَخسَرينَ أَعمالًا﴾

﴾qul hal nunabbi'ukum bi-l-'akhsarīna 'a'mālaⁿ⁻ⁱ﴿

﴾Say, 'Shall we inform you about the biggest losers in regard to works?﴿

﴿الَّذينَ ضَلَّ سَعيُهُم في الحَياةِ الدُّنيا وَهُم يَحَسَبونَ أَنَّهُم يُحسِنونَ صُنعًا﴾

﴾^alladhīna ḍalla sa'yuhum fī l-ḥayāti d-dunyā wa-hum yaḥsabūna 'annahum yuḥsinūna ṣun'aⁿ﴿

﴾Those whose endeavour goes awry in the life of the world, while they suppose they are doing good.'﴿[185]

Concepts Related To Happiness

People often confuse happiness and pleasure. They think happiness lies in pleasures only. This is a manifest error. Pleasure ends when its cause ends, whereas happiness exceeds pleasure. Happiness is

---

[185] Sūrat al-Kahf, Verses 103-104.

not a momentary, temporary thing. Although a person may feel happy while enjoying some pleasure, this could lead to wretchedness later. From Imām al-Ṣādiq ﷺ: "How often do short pleasures lead to long periods of sadness!"[186]

Harmony between Word and Deed

One of the most important causes of happiness is harmony between word and deed. A hypocrite experiences misery and guilt. God ﷻ said,

﴿يا أَيُّهَا الَّذينَ آمَنوا لِمَ تَقولونَ ما لا تَفعَلونَ﴾

⟨yā-'ayyuhā lladhīna 'āmanū li-ma taqūlūna mā lā tafʿalūnᵃ⟩

﴿كَبُرَ مَقتًا عِندَ اللَّهِ أَن تَقولوا ما لا تَفعَلونَ﴾

⟨kabura maqtan ʿinda llāhi 'an taqūlū mā lā tafʿalūnᵃ⟩

---

[186] Mufīd, Shaykh Muḥammad, *al-Amālī*, ed. Ḥusayn Ustād Walī, ʿAlī Akbar al-Ghaffārī, Beirut: Dār al-Mufīd, 1414/1993, 2nd ed., 42.

*{O you who have faith! Why do you say what you do
not do? It is greatly outrageous to God that you
should say what you do not do}*[187]

---

[187] Sūrat al-Ṣaff, Verses 2-3.